Selected Poems

Alan Stephens

SELECTED POEMS

Edited by A.A. Stephens

Dowitcher Press
Santa Barbara, California

Acknowledgments are given to the original publishers.

Copyright 2012 by A.A. Stephens

alanstephenspoems.com

Cover art: Tom Stephens
Book design and composition:
Valerie Brewster, Scribe Typography

ISBN 978-0-9857812-3-1 (hardback)
ISBN 978-0-9857812-2-4 (paper)

3 5 7 9 8 6 4 2
FIRST PRINTING

Dowitcher Press
www.dowitcherpress.com

For Fran

Contents

SONNETS FROM *Running at Hendry's*
(*In Plain Air,* 1982)

FROM *Water Among the Stones*
(1987)

Selected Poems

Small Song

"Turn on the hose," I say.
I kneel down on my lawn
To watch the water play.

At the depression where
The tree is set, it fills,
Transvisible as the air,

To level, tentative,
Then, trembling, overbreaks.
Its boundaries always give

Where the clear instants slow.
I stand, walk toward my house.
Shade slips. Place is aflow.

The Baby Cockatrice

I'd read of the vast reptiles, maybe seen
Some musty drawings of them, years ago.
The rumor that such creatures have once been
Will make a child fear, idly, *They are, now.*

Preoccupied and happy, I had fished
Well through a June day on Commotion Creek
And had my limit; now the water rushed
In shadow, mostly. Almost at the lake

I climbed the bank, tired, quiet. There he was.
He happened; total; there. He barely lay
A finger long—bone mouth and ruff and claws,
The plated body, and shock on shock, the eye.

And once I turned, all I had been stayed there
Whole in a gaze where no more could occur.

Be with me, powers
    of the tongue I love,

sources of clarity in
    the turns of life:

that the slow action of the
    understanding and the motions

of the rapid feelings
    breathe in unison—

health howsoever brief.

Hap

a picture postcard to my own boyhood

There is containment by small
brown mountains, by the Channel
waters that run in upon
the shores and sleek and litter
the sand; the pale firm islands
shut in the swarming lights and
cross-moves of the Pacific—

as if a topographic
ordering of the desires
lay ready; in season, low
clouds will form, and, thunderless,
come in changing rapidly,
set loose their spattering rains
and sweep off, torn by short winds—

the diversity of shore,
hill, and gorge is clarified
with stands of rough, bulbous oak,
a luminous sycamore
here and there, somberly thirst-
ing eucalyptus, mustard
washed yellow over the slopes—

nicely scaled for the human
eye, under a small soft sky
suggesting that, if you wished,
you might walk to what you see
anywhere here, observe it,
and make your way back during
the morning hours, through the trees.

Under the ordinary
bright gentle light of the place
I look in across a fence
at a bed of wild grasses
stippled with alyssum, with
a few native poppies—slight,
chill orange, snipped out finely.

A poppy is struggling
and the others barely shake;
one of its petals comes loose,
wavering down a kind of
creek of air. Son, you could choose
at such times to be happy,
yet free of your happiness,

knowing that its root is hap—
I'd have had you arriving
so as not to be bemused
in it; say, splashing ashore
as one of a colony
of Greeks fresh from disaster
who glance about expertly.

The Open World

I drive up on the headland
to campus, to finish
some last chores—down through the gaps
between the big buildings a
wind's coming in, clear, heavy,
coursing the Channel from the
open seas to the northwest.

It is cold—and could have crossed,
a week since, the Aleutians
from waters far back over
on the curving of the world;
it looks to be intently
cleansing this place of used air
in corners, of particles

on walks and in shrubbery;
students—of the few still here—
crossing between library
and dorm are minor figures
blown bare and vivid in the
strong sparkle of the light, the
bleakness is energetic

as I enter South Hall. But
the main switch has been thrown, the
windows locked tight—the air's dead
that had been well divided
and held in bright dry spaces

as of the mind itself, for
some feat of our attention—

as if a mind, having been
closed down, left a bitterness
suspended here—a mind grave
and perhaps magnificent,
that had again been failed of,
and was again awaiting,
fatefully, some dominion.

So a term's done; I hurry
and finish my chores, leaving
as if I'd been driven out
so as to meet with this wind—
an unoccupied roaring
inside my ears. At the tip
of the headland the sea is

racing and the eye plunges
and ascends alertly; and
the bottom of the sea, some
intricate system, surely,
as of conceptions left un-
tended, bears those contorted
currents and lashed surfaces.

Santa Barbara, California,
August–September, 1962

Second Evening

The sense of the real thirty years back in this clearness—
I could hold with my eyes, it seemed, the body
of the air; it was like standing at a fast stream
up in the mountains, seeing down through the water skin,

through the fine streakings of light, gripping in my vision
the whole crystalline heaviness of the water—clearness
right down to the toothed edges of the elm leaves,
almost black, stationary against the streaked colors

in the sky; cats emerged from under the granary, and taking
no notice of us, disappeared in high weeds; Seeley's Lake
started shining through the mild darkness; lights came on
near it, an uptilted glitter; heart's desire picked up.

About then I might stand up casually, half thinking
of those cats out in the weeds, and with hands in pockets
take a turn out on the lawn, and stop, and seem to myself
to be in the clear dark like a trout in its pool.

Later, air movement in the elm: night proper had begun.
One or two of us would rise, re-enter the house; and others
follow, I too, and meet in my turn, at the threshold,
the shock of the day's heat held still in the house.

Tree Meditation

πότνια ἀγλαόδωρ' ὠρηφόρε ...

—*ΕΙΕ ΔΗΜΗΤΡΑΝ*[*]

In this country, of the few
native trees the commonest
is the cottonwood. Settlers
planted it for windbreaks, for
shade; it grows in giant rows
on irrigation ditches,
and stands over the houses
shading them in the summer
all day; it grows in the draws
and in great dark glittering
groves on the North and South Platte.

It takes the classic tree shape—
a round symmetrical crown,
a trunk short and straight and thick;
up close, you see that the leaves
grow in loose swinging bunches
out on the periphery—
the interior is gaunt
and the few major branches
form powerful, still arches
that contrast with the quick leaves
throwing off sharp bits of light.

Considered thus, the whole thing
suggests perception combined

---

*From the closing lines of the *Hymn to Demeter,* referring to the lady
herself: 'Queen, giver of shining things, bearer of the seasons....'

with imperviousness. But
I turn to one specimen:
viewed up close its old trunk
with its deep rough crevices
and hard ridges covered with
sharp protuberances is
a badlands: there's nothing here
to penetrate to, it says;
impassive, unmoving, dead.

Whereas the leaves, with their fine
patterns and movements that take
the eye are transitory
and expendable—thousands
of them in agitation
all over, to the one trunk
almost featureless and like
nothing that's alive, whereby
the tree lives—holds out and lasts,
standing over the big ditch
steady and astir also.

The brown water runs past it
in the summer; in late fall,
the ditch dry and the weather
dry, the leaves turn a brilliant
clear yellow—it is startling,
the rough shining globe, against
the clear sky. The leaves fall then
in the ditch and are still bright

and new-looking when the snow
covers them, below the wood
that stands patient in the air.

The tree has had its full growth
for some thirty years at least,
bears its multitudes of seeds
regularly—small white dots
in cotton that expands vaguely
and goes aloft on breezes
looking supremely idle,
to drift up against fenceposts
and weeds and along the sides
of farm buildings and upon
the crops, irrelevantly.

The tree having grown from one
white dot, you know that of course
on the microscopic scale
in the seed's interior
it worked as distinctively
as it does here, fully grown—
below those microscopic
particulars, well below
the molecular, there lay
at last vagueness, though; vagueness
is ultimate. Thence it came,

thither doubtless it will go;
but here it stands out clearly

against a sky, it traffics
with the world intricately
and persistently, fastened
by many ways into things;
moving to the world's movements
its cotton drifting thickly
through the air on certain days
in midsummer is a sight
ordinary and solemn.

I spend half an afternoon
underneath this glistener:
in a light breeze the leaves make
a fine pattering sound, like
gravel sliding down a slope;
if the breeze strengthens, the sound
becomes a voluminous
general hissing; stronger still,
and the hissing becomes a
roar of massive excitement—
as if a cyclone had struck.

All these sounds are the sounds
of her present, passing, while
her trunk and limbs, hard things, dream
permanently, beneath sound
the dream of air and rock
and water, things around in
inorganic splendor.—Now
from the leaves I can tell how

at its quietest the air moves
in eddies, isolated
short currents, streams with dead spots …

Each leaf in a given bunch
is behaving differently;
none are the same size or shape,
all are versions; one flapping
while another seems to whirl
though in fact it oscillates;
another swings hectically
back and forth while its neighbor
hangs still; one flops over and
back, now, slowly; another
vibrates, the whole cluster sways.

I single out one leaf: it
begins to tremble, then wags
violently. The breezes
start, quit, and start up again
all afternoon. The musings
of the tree, on one calm day.
Now agitation up high;
below, not a leaf moves. Now
a breeze pours through the whole tree
and it rattles—the polished
leaves clash stiffly together.

Is all this movement purely
decorative. Is a leaf

normally agitated,
or still; or is this movement
needful to the tree's workings.
Are the movements troubles. Or
merely the life of the tree—
neither necessary nor
irrelevant; its queenly
life—not indifferent,
its impartial experience....

Three times I had the same dream
about this tree, in boyhood.
But I must explain—the trunk
for all its harshness, its lack
of fine structure, mere rocky
crevices and ridges, still
was vulnerable, of course—
a fungus got into it
near the point where the branches
arch up—the bark turned spongy
and brown, a depression formed.

The affliction seemed to me
dangerous; I was distressed.
A fluid like clean water
seeped from the place. Yesterday
when I examined the trunk
I saw clearly, down one side,
the stain left by the fluid;
though the spongy depression

had largely healed some time since,
in one spot I found some wet
soft bark; it smelt like moist earth.

That is the site of the dream.
I approach and a cavern
slopes upward into the huge
interior of the tree.
At the threshold I look up
and see on the crest in light
(a regular, clear nimbus)
a great deer standing quietly;
in the cave's natural dark
the deer is wholly visible.
It looks at me; its eye shines.

I have no inclination
to approach any closer;
according to the dream's plan
I've had a look at my life
which is all I was to do—
that was the feeling at first;
then the sense of the dream changed—
the deer was merely life
itself, being presented
in repose for a moment,
so that I could look at it.

So the tree stirs readily
in my mind—stirred yesterday

when I saw some of its kind
being felled a mile westward,
the great sections of the trunks
and limbs like fallen big game
in Africa—great females
slain and strewn about—but what
is this but an incident
I drove past the summer day
they fell in a solid world.

Underneath the tree, grasses—
bluestem, wild rye. A kind of
sharp-edged grass bends evenly,
as if combed, over the bank
of the ditch, trailing its tips
in the brown water. Woodbine,
planted by a bird dropping,
doubtless, grows here—it would come
from an old vine in the yard,
set out by some grandparent.
It is flourishing in here.

A pretty place. The milkweed
is blooming—clusters of dull
or dead pink flowers, spikey
petals set on a flesh-like
protrusion, a hole
opening in the center
shaped like a five-pointed star;
the sweet odor's attracting
not only bees but ants—large

black ants with legs that raise them
high off the ground. On the road,

close, cars pass. In the grass lie
small branches shed by the tree;
the bark on some has loosened
and come off with the passage
of the seasons, and the wood
is bleached out. A few of these
look like antlers. As I turn
to examine one of them
a funeral procession
passes—black Cadillacs, then
a long line of every-day cars.

They bear the dead and mourning
to the new cemetery
put in just beyond this farm—
the mourners preoccupied
matter-of-factly. I feel
like waving to them, but check
the impulse. The tree stands on
this thirty foot strip of ground
between the road and the field;
beyond, now, is not only
the graveyard but new houses.

So the traffic is heavy
on a road which in my youth
was silent, usually—
three or four cars going by

during a morning, perhaps.
Coming across on this ground
from the road, through the bluestem,
to see the wild geraniums,
I came close to cutting my foot
on a beer bottle fragment.

Still it is a pleasant place.
I notice along the base
of the great trunk a blackened
area—from an old weed fire,
I suppose. There is a weed
whose name I don't know—dark green,
tall, it too is blooming now—
greenish-white little flowers
in closely set clusters like
clover-blossoms.—Sacred ground,
as our life is not; and ground

inevitably profaned;
maybe inexhaustible,
too, in its way.—Yesterday,
cutting into a seed pod,
prodding it with the knife point,
hunting for the small white seeds,
trying to find some pattern,
I saw a small white spider
emerge from the packed cotton
and, while I watched, go racing
away across the table.

Elegy: The Old Man

Edging between the truck
and the wall I work back
to the far end, past the concrete,
onto the original dirt—
triangles of broken glass
shine among the old straw;
I make out a hame-ring,
yellowed and fly-specked; a mended
strap, cracked and with salt
from dried sweat still on it; high
on the wall, hung there
perhaps by my brother, to be visible
and out of the way,
an old 'silver'
harness buckle, a heart shape
set in the center, catching
the half-light where it bulges—
a bit of the bold old
finery of a set of harness.

I take it down. The heart is starred
with corrosion, dented on one side—
the whole buckle's bent awry,
across the concave underside
a spider has stretched a web:
in the quiet I can hear
the strain and give of the fabric
as I poke at it … nothing
underneath but a trace of fine
reddish dirt. I blow it out.

Regarding in the half-light
the heart's convexity, I consider
(in the heart's half-light)
taking the piece home with me....

The buckle and such scraps
are like the notions surviving
in the gaunt, brittle, half-dark
interior of an old man
and the barn an old man
lasting into this other world
maybe in a subdivision
in California: he has come out
to live with one of his children,
and runs the power mower
once a week. He actually
cuts the grass, the barn
really shelters a truck;

the old man finds himself
wearing a sportshirt,
the barn is carrying
in its inner flank a stack
of grease-gun cartridges.
The barn still holds the smell
of harness leather, and manure,
and feed and the like—faint,
dry, distant, the fragrance
persists like the manner
of an earlier day in the speech
of the old man.

My sons may never know
how satisfactory a place
a barn is to take a leak in,
and this is a barn, since you can still
do so, in the brown half-light,
the comfortable seclusion
—as for the dead in here,
I think of them long since busy
at burying their own, as I make my way
back out, toward the day-glare.

The Summer

The birds keep to their routines.
The big cottonwood glitters.
In the approaching heat
of the middle of the day
the elm makes little movements
now and then, like a dozing horse.

And on a distant county road
the sun bangs for an instant
on a windshield, flashing
like a signal; no reply.

A big butterfly, strongly
constructed, yellow with black
ribbing and trim, works the air
between the house and trees,
disappearing from time to time
around the corner of the house
or inside one of the trees,
reappearing abruptly.

I come out after breakfast
every day, and sit writing
in the morning shade. Clear hours!
Butterfly's in the foreground
frequently; tall dusty weeds
by the road; small house, trees, fields,
in the middle distance; then
the pale, vapory mountains.

If I look up from my page
the butterfly is often
the one moving thing in sight.
I watch him rise at the end
of a glide with a broken,
tottering movement, working
his way up to a high bough
then not alighting, but merely
poising in the air above it
and veering briskly off. Well,
he's not after anything.
A kind of extract of this
place, having worked free, he stays;

his apparently hesitant
turning this way and that is
just delighted watchfulness.

Afternoons he spends mainly
resting. And nights
on a weed stem, I suppose,
stiffening with the chill,
the stem knobbly with dew when
the morning sun first strikes it.

—suppose the words came in
the way a flight of blackbirds
I once watched entered a tree
in the winter twilight;
finding places for themselves
quickly along the bare branches
they settled into their singing
for the time.

To Fran

Out in the rain all afternoon
hands and neck chilled—
some trouble, anger

and late supper, the rain
smacking and clicking
outside the room

plenty of chablis
our sparse reflections
on the black window glass

where space comes pouring in
all the way in
from between the stars, in past the blacked-out moon—

desolately it enters the room
and streams around your shoulders
without harm—how curious—

and enters my grizzled beard
stopping when it arrives
at the skin warmth—

~

it must be we belong in it—at once remotely
and intimately; the way a sheepherder's fire at night belongs
in the distance on a desert upland

The White Dog Truth

I make out the white bulk in the dark—
the dog approaches at a quick pace
and goes by showing no interest in me,
and such is the quiet of the street
I hear the clicking of his toenails
on the blacktop, quick, business-like,
even half a block away, the sound
growing fainter very gradually
and already, while I keep an eye
on the wire-thin half rim of light
the moon shows in a sky jagged
with trees along the bottom—
already this encounter, the white bulk passing
in the dark, the diminishing click
of the toenails along the stretch
of silence back there, cannot be forced
not to have been, the lords of creation
themselves will have to submit to
its having been, if they should find it
some day blocking the way of a desire.

Variation from a Theme by Marsden Hartley

Hartley, summer was plainly for you,
    remarker of joined clearnesses, plover noticer,
    savorer of 'infant clams' and campestris, among the opulence,
    'the look of bright everlastingness'

But it is not for me, in summer
    it seems there's nothing to do
    but continue what's become obvious, greens
    overlapping soberly, whitening sky,
    stationary August.

An upper rocky field, and the way
    begins to open, a few bright
    stubble stalks leaning among the clods, nearby,
    and red light flickering in the distance, on the blue flats
    where they're burning off the cattails in the sloughs,

And 'shall the cold flowing waters
    that come from another place
    be forsaken?'—I'm on my way
    up to a wind-swept place
    of darkness, snow, and some lights, and further on
    a granite cave, icy water on its walls
    black flecked with white and pink, the good
    lair dark I dream to; start down fresh from.

Desert

This bad country in the late afternoon wears us down,
The rocks with their dead purples,
The scabby cactuses, trees with tiny oily leaves

And thorns so big they're visible from the road,
Shrubs that look made out of old wire. Finally it all says:
That hard life of yours couldn't live out here, the bad country

Would free you of it; then the spirit, turning
Ruthless as it was in the days of the anchorites,
Could have a respite and stand empty on some hillside.

Moon, Rain

Homeward, and how sudden
The round white moon
Above the winter poplars
(Bunches of broomstraws)
And the gray
Of the sky in that quarter
A silence for the moon statement
And she is indoors at this hour
And the moon not visible anyway
From down in the canyon
This was yesterday—
Today where she is, at the window
Rainy light on the faucet chrome
And on the sheath of wet
On the tree, the bare
Apricot the rain sparely decorates
A knop of silver
Here and there, before
The window where she is

Various Presences

Coming back to the house through the dark
I see a flashlight come on
at the dark window of Tim's room—
as I enter he trains it on me
and greets me.

He has climbed out of his bed
to look at some tomato worms again
which he put in a can today with fresh tomato leaves
fragrant with the scent
of tomatoes themselves—
he explains: he could hear the worms
chewing the leaves in the dark,
he imitates the sound for me,
a slight sucking sound.

The broad scars or scabs
on tomatoes are made, I suppose,
by these worms. We sit a moment
watching them in the flashlight beam.

Big fellows, a clear, light green,
built high and rectangular
like boxcars, and with a thorn
like a rose thorn set in their hind ends;
on their flanks are stripes,
diagonal, crooked, black with white edging;
between each stripe is an imitation eye—
we look at it, it looks back at us,

a clear black pupil
rimmed with a delicate white tissue
that makes the eye appear to glisten
with moisture. The expression, we decide,
is that level, considering regard
you meet in the eye of a toad
or a lizard.

Late to Pray

All around the infrequent little towns
(a few gaunt old stores still in business,
elm-dark residential streets half-way
abandoned, a broken-hearted silence in them)
lies the shining wheat country, gold white
and open, all visible or else nothing;
hill gleams above hill to the smooth rim
of the horizon like the sight of excellence itself.

If you are still holding out here, every street
an elm tunnel opening at either end on the dazzle—
in the afternoon silence all the bright grain
standing motionless takes on a distant look;
and is again a goddess, with child,
and absorbed in that, in being nothing more.

Scribbling Poems on a Visit Home

Poor little bastards, is
no provision being made
for their future?

They just scatter like beans—
the pod splits and curls back
spring-like, and out they fly

during these dry August afternoons
while the tremendous, dazzling thunderheads
white as the original white

of creation, build up in the west
like the springtime fathers that drenched
fields they knew not at all,

and passed through never to return.

August 27, 1967

A Day in the Back Country

I

Strong cold gusts rake the ridge;
I drive into the east light;
The roadside wild oats shake,
Glisten delicately
—Silver for a girl's wrist.
But here sea haze to right,
Mountain chasm to left,
Against their small clearness.

II

Miles, and nobody, then
Two helicopter crews,
Machines idling nearby,
And this whole back country
Seems theirs—they criss-cross it
As they please, their faces
Interested, easily
Looking out over it.

III

More miles, and I wonder
Am I lost? A deer stands
Quietly in the road,
A flowering up, it seems,
Of the dust of the road
At just this moment,
And the road itself wild.
The deer walks off, down the slope.

IV

Down steep, tight curves, jolting.
A strange rattle starts up
In the steering column.
Mudholes from the oozings
Of roadside springs. And there,
The shine of the river
Winding in the open
Valley. And no one down there.

V

Much of that day is gone.
Half careless as I was
Of it—since it was mine,
I chose that, rather than
Become cautious with it;
So, much of it's well gone—
Into my bones, maybe;
Certainly out of reach.

VI

Sycamores and alders,
Grass turning a bright brown;
In the vertical light
The loud water ablaze,
Skimmed by green-backed swallows—
Hawk, black in the distance,
Calling down at it all—
Now from these I recall:

How in the unknown
River with nothing
Promised came the jolt
And quiver of the
First trout (thereafter
How readable were
The pools and riffles!)—
How then I kept on
Fishing past lunch time
Knowing the fatigue
This would mean; then ate
Somewhat hurriedly
At last with my boots
On a log to dry—
How I went downstream
Barefoot, astonished
By the pain! each small
Rock made its own pain—
How slowly that pain
Drove back the idea
Of a pleasant walk
Barefoot to that pool
Downstream; how I caught
Two fine trout while each
Move I made meant pain;
How the log had spurs
On it, like pinpoints,
Entering my bare feet
When I came back; how
In midafternoon,

Tired, I took my last
Good trout, at a bend
In dark blue shadow,
Under a rock ledge;
How then I rested
In some tall grasses,
How they hissed loudly
With the gusty wind
While I on the ground
Lay in still air; how
I thought of sleep, slept;
And woke in changed light,
Glare and shadow strange
On the water—late
Afternoon now! How
Fishing back upstream,
Seeing the water
From the other way—
Alien—chilled me;
How in my fatigue
I went by riffles
I'd have fished, before;
How in that estranged
New-shining water
I caught two more trout,
And, leaving them cleaned
On a streamside rock,
Turning back found one
Moved—then saw the snake
That moved it, his jaw-

joints unfastened, whole
Head of fish inside
His mouth, his own head
Startlingly deformed,
Eyes looking close-set
Now that the small head
Had been stretched so wide;
How, motionless, he
Watched me, knowing well
That I might kill him,
How his eyes asked, "Well,
Will you?" and waited;
How, as I held still,
He moved, ever so
Slightly, stealthily,
Looking right at me.
How I went upstream
And from being tired
Lost three lures in quick
Succession, thinking:
I'm skin-tight, aching
With this day, bone-cracked
By it, like my friend
The snake with my trout
All but disabled
By the good fortune.
—Time to crawl home, then,
And sleep it off. How
A big, bushy-tailed
Ruddy coyote paused

On a stony spur
And watched me a moment
As I drove toward him
On the road out; how,
Truth to say, the sight
On my return, of wife
And sons distressed me
—I distressed myself
Among them, come back down
As I was, unfit
For human converse,
Drunk with the dry, bright
Liquor of the day.

The Heavily Watered Whiskey
of This December Sunlight

… if time is friend
or enemy? we stand still
by going and go
standing still:
along a hillside this
midwinter afternoon,
"An old thing to be doing"—what?
"Filing down a trail like this,"
I tell her, the pleasure of it
that we are partly roused ancestors, or
as if we were an old trellis
with a young vine in it
where now the air is moving
birds visit the grapes
the season lives
a sunny and windy freshness
so ancient—this
or nothing for us.

Thinking of Roethke

by the McKenzie one evening

To the heaven of ideas I should prefer
A heaven of events, such as Roethke knew,
Or so I think as I watch the McKenzie running
Fast and smooth, blue-green to where a rock
Jolts it into a tumult, uprearing, clear white,

Surging and surging (and louder, it seems) as night
Advances. Well, Roethke, dead now about a year,
Leaned quietly to heed places like this one.
I light the Coleman, the near boulders and fir trunks
Are suddenly cloven—black shadow, flat white light,

And a jumpy glitter on the black current that shows
Between the trunks. Sticks in my little fire
Redden and bend. The time passes. It passes; quiet.
How plainly I am here, in this flat glare.
The world is some kind of concentrate, clearly.

A mayfly, delicate green, high-winged, alights
Awkwardly on my arm—from a long stay under the river,
Through many moltings, the thing has come up
For the air and the light: ephemerid; 'ephemeria
Phroneontes.' It flies off smartly into the dark.

Things are faithful. The fir trunks in silence, in it
Like reeds in a pool, the river jarring against its rock,
The small hot fire, the vivid and matter-of-fact insect—they
Take place, a deep relief, as I look around to see
With Roethke in mind a last time before turning in.

ABOUT THE DESTRUCTION OF SOULS AND SELVES

… Then flush the world in earnest. Let yoursel' gang,
Scour't to the bones, and mak' its marrow holes
Toom as a whistle as they used to be
In days I mind o' ere men fidged wi' souls,
But naething had forgotten you as yet,
*   Nor you forgotten it.*
— HUGH MACDIARMID
PRAYER FOR A SECOND FLOOD *

Piah
(PART I)

Is a self
so precious, Piah? I think sometimes
a self is an unnecessary growth, a kind

of wart, at best
harmless, not too unsightly—irritated
it will grow troublesome, at last maybe malignant.

Or sometimes it is
an instrument, to be rightly proud of,
that works well, is even perhaps attractive and amusing—

**Toom* is *empty, fidged* is *moved.*

or even an article
of some elegance and beauty; to be
dismantled or discarded, though, if it becomes

in 'this world of fleeting
trials and choices,' out of place
or out of date, a piece of outsize bric-a-brac—I know selves

that should be, like some great
and now elaborately ugly Nootka woodcarving,
propped in the ethnic room of a dusty provincial museum....

But commonly a self
is a more modest thing, something improvised
by the spirit, over a stretch of some years, for daily use—

use that's no easier
on it than on any other implement;
scratches, corrosion, dented and mended places in time

may give it its pathos
and dignity—some old carpenter's tool, handle
broken and taped, blade nicked but smooth and bright still.

All this says nothing of
the temporary selves made for special
occasions, and sound and true for their purposes,

or of that self of selves
which is like those marine creatures
made up of different animals, no one kind

able to survive apart,
each kind providing in its own way
for all the others—a Portuguese man-of-war of a Self!…

Jack

In photographs the light flashes
        Off his big cheekbones
Which are as definite as fists
        While his eyes flash
With their different light, looking out
        At the quick, hard
Movements of his own world.
        He is not a sufferer.

Sure of himself, for the reason
        That he has thought out
And made for himself—made by hand
        You could say—a weapon of a self,
A self for hard use. He named
        Himself—Nicaagat,
Who appeared from out of the desert westward
        One spring, and joined the Utes.

Some say he had White blood, some
        That he was part Mexican
Or Paiute or Apache. Sold as a boy
        By the Ute chief Walkara
(The one who castrated the boys he sold
        To Navajos for placid herdsmen)
To a Mormon family. They raise him—take him
        To church, send him to school.

Get him a job: six months
        Driving an ice wagon
In Salt Lake City and he vanishes

To reappear the Ute
He remained to the end. Such a man
    And the world are brothers wrestling.
He does not forget which of the two of them
    Is the elder and will win.

Be a Ute for all you're worth.
    Marry a Ute wife,
Take your people each year into the mountains
    For the hunting, summer and fall;
Trading and (no purist) rations in winter;
    Fight the Sioux (with Crook—
'Jack's callous ferocity startled
    Even Crook's veterans');

Dance the Bear Dance, dance
    The war dance and sing
Its one word song the tribe name
    tsiuta all night long,
Slow the Whites down with words:
    You come see about dis.
Why all dese soldiers want to see too?
    Ain' no trouble dere.

You come. I show you Meeker
    Ain' beat up. Lot of soldier
Come to Agency, women get scared,
    Children get scared,
Young men maybe dey want to fight.
    Old ones say No fight,

But maybe young men don't hear
        Old men—then trouble.

When the troops come on anyway
        Slow them down with bullets.
And when more troops come on
        Use words once more, gain a month,
Gain half a year…. When the tribe
        Is driven out at last
From its country, when the Ute self's broken,
        Not to break along with it.

No, be separate again, be one Ute,
        If that is possible—a teamster
Once again. Then some soldiers, questions
        And a sudden argument
About a horse theft and 'Jack was wounded
        As he ducked into a teepee.
When the soldiers pulled down the teepee
        Jack ran into another.'

I remember him by what it took to kill him.
        'He was protected from our bullets
By bales of robes and rawhides.
        He fired his carbine and killed
Sergeant Casey. I then caused a shell
        From a mountain howitzer
To be fired into the teepee in which Ute Jack
        Was barricaded, killing him.'

A Bundle of Colorow's Things

HIS PIPE

It lies in a glass case,
the bowl cut from red stone
rubbed smooth, the stem
carved of some pale wood.
on the stem's upper surface
a tortoise, a deer's head,
two ears of corn
laid side by side, and
the head of a mountain goat,
all in a row, spaced evenly
in high relief, each detail
clear-edged. From the dead
air of the case the pipe
calls up in its workmanship
a carver hunched with his knife
on a sunny winter morning
in a quiet so intent
he does not know he is happy.

HIS PICTURE

A huge face. Wide heavy cheekbones
and big hacked-out looking nose,
tired intelligent glittery eyes —
glittery as black grease. A sharp-cut
straight wide sulking mouth.
Beneath the lower lip and the cheekbones
emphatic black shadow, counterpart
of the light aglare against his forehead.
A willful face, an eager face.

COLOROW IN *THE DENVER POST*

In '88, the year before he died:
'The Whites have asked for Colorow's removal
And the latter persists in staying on the ground.
He is by nature ugly and mean-tempered
And cannot be scared off or bluffed away.
This, coupled with his notion that he owns
The land, which has become a passion with him,
Has made it very unpleasant, and at times
Dangerous for the settlers.'

HIS SMALL JOKE IN A UTE COUNCIL

…The old man said to the whites:
All right, we give you some land
For your presents, only
You must take it away with you.
We do not want your land
Lying around over our country.

HIS ANCESTRY

His father was
a Comanche, his mother
a Jicarilla Apache.

WHAT SOME SAID HAPPENED TO HIM ONE DAY

> Carl Adams, the man
> who was born Karl Schwanbeck,
> kicked Colorow downstairs
> for waving a revolver
> and calling the Governor
> liar, damn liar, goddamn liar.

WHAT HE DID AT MILK CREEK

When the soldiers crossed over
the Reservation line, the Utes
met their advance and stopped it.
And then Colorow, the clown
with the enormous belly,
showed the Utes the way to hold
the soldiers inside the pits
they had dug when caught in the open —
hold them there breathing the stench
of their own dead horses,
and no water, tasting their own sweat
in the glare of the hot sand-flat.

MR. WOLF LONDONER'S COLOROW STORY

When I kept store in California Gulch
Colorow used to come in for some trading,
And I'd ask him to dinner, being afraid
If I didn't he might take our scalps. One time
He came with five squaws, and they ate and ate.

Colorow'd take a spoonful of soup, and spit.
Spit alongside the table, a villainous thing,
But I durst not say a word. When they were finished
Colorow mumbled something in Indian
And one of the squaws gave a buckskin to my wife.
She hardly knew what it was or what to do with it.
I was in the office later when Colorow
Came back. He was a terribly big Ute —
Blocked out the light and darkened the whole front.
He stood there holding his stomach with both hands.
I was a little afraid, about the dinner.
He said, 'Heap sick.' I said, 'Been drinking whiskey?'
'No, eat too much. Want doctor.' — 'Doctor's gone,'
I told him. He said, 'You give me medicine.'
Now I was kind of scared. I did not know
But what he would go for me. I thought the best
I could do would be to give him some Epsom salts.
I knew it wouldn't kill him. I got a cup
And filled it, nearly, and he had a hard time
To get it down, and had to take a great deal
Of water with it. Then he went away.
Next morning, going down to the gulch
For a pail of water, I met my friend coming up.
He must have weighed 275, usually,
But now he looked like an umbrella cover.
We stopped, I thought I had better face the music.
'No good. White man heap bad.' — 'Why, Colorow,
What is the matter?' — 'Pretty near die. Want doctor.'
I helped him up to the store. Then I fetched the doctor,
And when I told him what the trouble was,

He said, 'How much did you give him, for ___ sake?'
'I gave him a tin cup full,' I said. He said,
'Why that was enough to kill an elephant.'
'Well,' said I, 'it hain't killed Colorow.'

~

  … Everybody's Indian,
  Even the Indians',
  Old many-souls!
  How many times
  Defeated (and the soul —
  That temporary product
  Of an obstructed spirit —
  Discharged like a breath, and the mind
  Gone oddly quiet, as in
  The aftermath of a burst of rage),
  Only to turn up elsewhere
  Unexpectedly
  In full force
  To the end, with the old
  Abrupt talent
  For getting into action!

  To die of old age
  In your own lodge,
  And on the White River
  (Oh, far downstream, in Utah) —
  Of the many souls
  This last one, so light,

Like a puff of smoke!
Going up in stillness
Out of the hacked-out
Huge old self, that had been
So much photographed
For the papers;
That had supplied them,
And the Utes, also,
With the materials
For so many stories;
And that was a good, workable
Ute self, now
Lying still for once,
And solid, heavy; yes,
As if it had been fashioned
With chisel and hand axe
From a tree trunk.

Ouray

A clear mind
and a liking for action.

When the brother of his wife Chipeta
tried to kill Ouray with a knife, for giving up

Ute land in a treaty,
Ouray broke the man's wrist and threw him in a ditch.

~

There being Whites
by the hundreds of thousands out here

and Utes
by the hundreds, to place the obvious

first, each time
he thinks, is his solitary distinction, and

crushing a Ute,
compromising with a White

impartially,
in honor of that first thought,

telling lies
to White commissioners, without hesitation

expelling the old chief
his adoptive father, when the old man would not

deal with the Whites—
what are these but tesserae in his mosaic

integrity
whom it suited Ute and White to call corrupt.

He had for company
Chipeta and his own accurate thinking.

~

In group photographs
it's always Ouray that sits, hands on knees, front and center,

fully there, solid,
alert, his gaze direct and ready to meet

with full attention
the attention of anyone looking at him here

as of—right now:
it is an expression that doesn't yield *anything*.

And let me in these Shades compose
Something in Verse as true as Prose.
—POPE

Autumn: Island

after Jorge Guillén

Autumn, an island
with a severe
profile, watches the combers with their crests
that waver, race forward
to their glistening destruction.

A love for line, and
the grapevine is stripped
of its overlapping green

and a small basket
filled with clusters
out of—good luck: sealed in them
a balancing of dreams
about things possible.

From secret high spirits
a clean style; wisdom the more definite
as it becomes the more inconspicuous, a plain
branch above the hurrying colors.

The Fall Plowing Back Home

Young, and I burned the world away
Ahead of me, anywhere I went,
With my personal blaze.

Now the world is filling back in.
How I like the plain details,
Complete with shadows, in the low sunlight.

When did I empty?—it's as quiet in here
As a cobweb furred with dust.
Let the harness on its peg

Harden, let the green build up
On the battered brass knobs of the hames.
This old manure scent is dry, and very fine.

Long blades of the afternoon
Slope in through the drop-siding,
Slit the dimness. The light wind

Of late afternoon carries clearly
The fly-buzz of a whole fleet
Of tractors, over the flat brown fields.

The Man of Feeling

Let it go on, he says,
The sweet, steady humming
Of time, and leans again
In the light of the lamp, outside
The gray and dripping day,
Its light entering the window and setting
Its pewter-colored shine
on the back of his hand, his books
In reach, the three or four people
He loves best, at their own doings
In the near middle distance
Of his life this wintry day
As he enters his fiftieth year,
Let it go on,
That sweet hum, let there be
No end to it, ever.

~

Curious how ready he is to die
At moments when he looks around
Quite happy with things—driving
Through town this afternoon,
Heading home, looking forward
To dinner and the evening with *her*,
The town so pleasant in the clear, late light
Reflected from the white undersides of clouds
Pushing out over the rooftops
From the mountains, the air
Chill, fresh off the ocean—

At Los Olivos and Alameda Padre Serra

Below St. Mary's retreat
In its greenery, on its hill,
Are some unowned olive trees
Backed by a stone wall
In a crook of the busy street.
You can visit them when you please.

Though trucks gear down and brake,
Growling and hissing, and cars
Whoosh by the place all day,
The light's clear there, the gray
Grove whitens, when it stirs,
As if for its own sake,

The ground is packed and bare
And stained bright purple and black
From the unpicked bitter fruit
That spurt from underfoot.
Walking, I do not lack
For quiet in that air.

~

Winter dusk, and I peer
From the stone bridge nearby
Through alder and sycamore
At the stream racing high
And red with mountain mud
And listen till I hear
Under the water-roar

The streambed boulders thud
And see them gone dead white
and silent at this spot,
And the last pool sunk from sight,
And the clear, weightless current
Of the air quivering hot
Over the solid torrent.

~

A place being manifold
With more than the eye can hold,
Was I once Spanish or Greek
To like these gray trees so—
Or a solitary kid
From the dusty plains,
Much to wonder about
Inside himself and out,
Sent to school in town,
Shown a few things to know,
While, in a country drowse,
All but completely lost—
Who came at last to seek
Clearness in all he did,
And had for all his pains
The thing in itself clear
And the meaning disappear
—A strange curse to bring down
On much that he loved most;
Latterly come to stray

Under these twisted boughs
Of the old wisdom, where
Mixing leaves with air
Off the sea below
This is what they say—
Σοφία first was skill,
What a craftsman knew,
Physician, sculptor, smith,
And it is so still,
Being just a way
Not a thing to keep
Or a state of mind
That we stiffen with
And go slowly blind—
But an act of mind
In the course of being,
Going with our seeing;
To sit still and know
Is itself to do,
In our moving through
With the rest of things;
Standing here, we go,
Passing we stand still
(So the gray grove sings
Whitening on its hill)
Till at last we see
Or rather, learn to guess
In our doubleness,
That awake we sleep,
Sleeping we're awake,

And all these mixtures mean
That no thing can be
For its own sweet sake;
Clearness has its source
In the Vague and Vast—
Shapeless, these two last,
While clearness's green leaf
Shapely bright and brief
Consummates their powers;
That the seen and unseen
Send into each other
One another's force,
Separated die
Quicker than cut flowers—
As for what you write
(Rustles one old tree)
Why, Athene knows
Every poem goes
No matter at what height
Over rails of prose,
Length on length on length
Shoved by smoky strength
Straight and smooth and bright,
And the ugliness
Where the iron is mined
Of necessity
Has a dignity
She could not but bless
—If she, brought to birth
by Hephaestus' axe,

Shouting her war cry,
And without a mother,
Were the blessing kind.

~

Such is what I heard
When the branches stirred
In their dialect;
Now I look around
And this bare dry ground
Prompts me to reflect
No man walks beside
Athene the clear-eyed,
She was born complete
Of the bright-lit myth
Where she keeps her distance
From the shadowed earth;
From the twisted trees
Standing here, for instance,
Catching the sea breeze—
Slow to grow and bear,
Whether here or elsewhere
Cultivated stocks
Grafted to the wild
(Mixture in the shoot)
Able to hold out
For the dusty farmer
Through the longest drought,
Grappled in the rocks;

The black, bitter fruit
Yielding a clear oil
That once symboled human
Plenty and good will,
Bitter turning mild
In the hands of skill
For the kind of peace
Households need—all this
Sponsored by a woman
Who was born in armor
And who bore no child.

Mid-October

And such
things as he achieved are
to him now as its ringed
wood to an old tree, firm
and of the essence
and utterly remote
from the present quick
movements of the leaves, whereas
from the most recent
of a varied assortment
of misjudgments in the life
the pain is as keen
as it is familiar, joining
the life's quite particular
griefs that, subsiding of course
in time, run fresh nevertheless
as when, years back,
they arose, while it is now, now
with the first cold wind
of the fall blowing
down the empty road
that he's walking, one more
aging man, lights
from the house windows
piercing now here now there
the wind-roughed trees,
the first leaves
to be torn loose in the season
skidding wildly past him,
he gaining the hilltop,

looking across the canyon
at the mountain, trickling
headlights along its road,
the trees roaring now and
dark below, their wrenching
tops catching the red
of a last flare of the sunset.
No car passes. Nobody else
out here. The wind hurries
its new, clean, cold volumes of air
through the big vacancy between him
and the mountain: old elation,
come of this icy freshness
in things in their clearness,
shapes—in the sharp air
of this one deepening dusk—black
now and unreturning,
though a man travels
no more than a tree.

Night Piece

Last night I lay awake
beside my sleeping wife
at four a.m., and listened:
wind sifted through the pine tree
and made a branch tip finger
the roof above our bed
as if reflectively.
Then I went in my mind
the way the wind was taking—
down through the winding canyon,
shouldering past the trees,
and onto Hendry's beach,
across the channel waters,
gaining the channel islands,
and then the open sea
and moving by itself
over the dark swells
and nothing more to seek.

~

My dear slept on beside me
I knew; I had for proof
her light breath on my cheek.
The branch kept fingering
the same place on the roof.

A Puff of Smoke

When my old friend writes to me
Of the 'stark fact that the mind
Appears to be infinite
And to have nothing to do
With the scientific "law"
Of dispersion'—I don't know,
I'll have to write in reply,
Maybe it is infinite
As the world of numbers is,
His purlieu. Immortal, though?
Why, it's an activity,

And it stops. Smashing the skull
Ends it—the anesthetist
Interrupts it, telling you
Mildly, 'Let me see how wide
You can open your mouth, now,'
And the next thing is a flood
Of bright gray light, followed not
By immersion in darkness,
But a moment's consciousness
That the light's gone; and then
Not even darkness. Nothing.

What is this nothing? Nothing.
Where is this nothing?... Think how
When a reader finishes
His reading, as an event
Of his attention, it is
A memory—a different
Event. His book's an object,

Gathers dust among objects
In no terrible darkness
Or emptiness, but only
In things around, continuing.

There are no gaps in the world.
If spirit's intermittent,
A flickerer that at last
Goes out, the body goes on,
Disintegrating only
To other bodies. The fine
Chemicals...! (While the body
And its habitat were what
Spirit had burned for its warmth
And light. In the beginning,
Spontaneous combustion.)

~

—Conscious again; shaking, cold,
Interstellar cold sunk in
To the middle of the bones.
No doubt from the shock. A new
Numbness down there, and fresh pain,
And a meek feebleness, and
Morphine, all teach the spirit
How it sits reliantly,
Precariously, astride
Its old mule, the body, now
Tottering along strange roads.

I am still musing upon
The horrors that shape themselves
In the gray country of drained
Vitality, foul places
And presences that we two
Innocents visited, with
A sighting one night (eyes closed)
Of death's door, going past it
In the hospital basement:
Bare concrete, tall, wide, unmarked,
Set flush in the concrete wall.

~

The stunned spirit monitors
The shocked and wounded body
And itself; and puzzles how
The mind includes the body
The body includes the mind
Equally.
            —I remember
Using the body the way
One drove a car when a kid:
To see what it could take, from
A curiosity quite
Disinterested, from anger

At a world so impassive
And clearly uninterested
In the spiritual (no
We would not have used that word),

Authority of energies
Our own yet not our own; and
From exuberance.... When young
We are I think but distantly
Attached to our bodies, being
Ill-informed still on any
Necessity we live by.

Years pass and we sink into
The body. Now warily there
I find I take a kindly
Interest in the more or less
Faithful old mount (that is
When fairly healthy), wrily
Admiring its survival
Of pain sickness and danger,
With recollections of work,
Food, sleep, love, talk; of places
Where for moments all was well.

And one day we are body,
And nothing more. Though spirit
Is instructed by the body
Not the other way around,
It's in the spirit only
That instruction can take place
—Of what grand elaborate sorts—
While a definition of
The body might be: What knows,
Really knows its lessons, so
Is a fully accredited

Member of the cosmos. While
The spirit, born ignorant
Of its own rules, and the world's,
At the end has, at best, earned
Only a provisional,
Temporary membership,
Still more ignorant than not
(Which must befit it, must be
Of its nature)—and at worst
Will be all but blackballed (yet
Never quite, even at worst?)....

~

Home again! I write my friend,
And at such a time as this—
To be driven home and see
On the way people's fruit trees
Bright with blossoms in back yards;
And on the hills above town
New green from the recent rains
After a dry winter; that
Was a piece of good timing
I tell you; and once at home
Green fresh outside the windows.

~

Still, what the wan spirit knows,
After its late adventures,
Is a world surrounding it
As nicely put together,
And frail, as the seed crown of
A dandelion; and I walk,
Gaining strength, the grassy hills
Through the wildflowers, little
Fire shapes in the green, fading
Here and there with the approach
Of summer, and its routines.

First Deposition

A trout stream in the high Rockies,
my wife's laughter, a little brass whale
from Taiwan, the sight from my study window
of the two blue hills above the trees,
all kinds of cats, the high desert
of northern Nevada, all particulars
concerning the life and writings of Pope,
the time of sundown and just after,
the grammar of any language, a flawless
sea urchin shell found on Hendry's beach
and kept around and looked at
almost daily for ten years now,
all the birds, the look of Greek on the page,
cottonwood trees in summer, glistening
above the ditches in the dry country
of the west, the words of English songs
of the period 1580 to 1620,
the smell of lumber, of the iron
in a hoe as you file it, of a horse;
bolts of fine woolen goods;
the Indian head nickel; rain,
snow, sunshine, wind, darkness,
the game of poker, discovering used bookstores
in large cities, the clear recollection
of the house and farmyard of early childhood;
driving through streets to meet someone
at the airport, at an hour, late or early,
when you are not usually out; bare trees;
the rhythms of iambic trimeter;
granite boulders; coffee; the coming
of the early darkness of December.

Pure Perception

And I woke up this morning
    To nothing on my mind.
Friends, it was putting to your ear a watch
    You had forgot to wind.

It was walking through the half-dark
    Of a sales barn after the sale;
Litter and echo; light from a far door
    Falling still and pale—

Was the barren clarity
    Of a February sun
And you look up at a stony peak and see
    That the stone is stone.

O all day long the air
    Will move clear, cold, and thin
Over things that have come up too near to me—
    It will razor off my skin,
    And no event within.

The Gnomes

Months pass and still
they come squeezing out—
little deformed pre-poems
between crammed duties
and whatnot, the attention
wrenched this way and that.

Keeping their distance
they look at me
with their lopsided faces, one eye
higher than the other,
in those eyes the light,
a pale, clear green,
of an unworldly
wisdom; they stand there quietly
for as long as I look at them.

Work

And I wake up,
yeh, it is dawn,
the young helper, waiting
pale and serious
outside the window.

Late Song: Ambush

I see my bones lie white
And shining in the Light,
I need the darkness here
Inside me to repair
Old purposes much frayed,
Or shelved, being so ill-made,
Parts of my life now broken
For clear thoughts left unspoken,
Things I uttered, too,
Made some of it run untrue,
Of all that's mine alone
Little fit to be shown—
With more work crowding in,
A fresh page to begin,
And a recent bad mistake
To fix, lest the Light break
And my case still not made,
My meanings all waylaid,
And all I am lying clear
With no interior,
And my bones sprawled out white
And shining in the Light

Second Deposition

Sometimes I look inside
and see a mountain slope
in Colorado. There
my grief comes trickling down
from the packed snow of my hate
freshly, spring after spring,
through darkness under fir trees.

You've seen such places, maybe.
There breed the little wild trout,
the brooky and the cutthroat
in their icy brilliant colors,
there, under branches sagging
or broken from the snows,
the thin song of mosquitoes
criss-crosses the chill air,
there, tiny colored stars
on the dark of the wet moss,
a few mountain flowers tremble,
fine roots washed in snow water,
the colors clear and cold
—almost too small to notice
should you stray under there,
certainly too small to pick.

And These

Out of an occasional delight
in those icy vacancies
that stretch away
from the 'comforting stench
of comrades'
          mostly
of a simple, bi-partite
structure like the fungus
living with an alga
to make a lichen, some
2,000 species of which
inhabit the Arctic, fastened
to rocks, pieces of bone,
cast-off antlers, so cold
and barren and dark
their situation, some of them
may grow only during one
day in a year—in the long
darkness each bright patch
holding fast to its object.

Five O'Clock

Just before hitting the turn
and entering the down ramp
hunched up and tensed again
and the little new moon in the west
by herself in the early darkness
cocked backward so jauntily
on the steep downward slope
into the wintry ocean

Dec. 19, 1975

85

A malformed and much sophisticated world
it is, and I in my fiftieth winter of it
with a few ordinary things known, matters of doing,
matters of desire, and there's the full moon
in the workshop window again,
with its old silent abruptness, light
held cleanly inside its firm rim,
lifting so clear and cold
over the wintering poplars—scrawny
columns of brush upfountaining
through how many years? over
the worn and frozen lawn, grove
and grass burning white together

A Young Slug on the Counter

Brought in unawares—suddenly
Airborne as he was clambering
Over the *Times* in his cruise
Across the rainy sidewalk
In the early November dark.

And now on the move again,
Singlemindedly, belongingly,
In the warm lit kitchen,
His rain-freshened, mucusy skin
Glistening, clean as the porcelain tiles;

And meanwhile, to imagine, still
Travelling through his tissues
Toward the immaculate dark
At his center, the phosphorus-cold glow
Of his wonder: shy, by itself, slow.

In the Canyon

More distinct
than ever we

can be,
their ways

remotely
crisscrossing ours,

gods
each

with his one
virtue

(or maybe two
or three)

by itself
simple,

disclosed
with such unintended

sureness and
so glancingly

passing across
the eye-piece

of our
complicated and

clumsily aimed
attention

~

Of birds the big flicker
his cry from a treetop clanging
in the first light: how to begin.
And the deer, for the body's lightness, surprised
at mid-day, russet and a hint of antlers
over the green bushes then gone,
as if he had not been in motion but hanging there
when the whole forest shifted a little
and concealed him—
the bear for knowledge
in detail—there is no other—of his terrain, and
for his unhurried gait
that takes him so rapidly
where he wants to go, his company
his solitariness—and for his capacious
robe of sleep for the long cold and darkness,
and in the new grass by the footpath out back
the green and yellow striped
garter snake that shows every time
how innocence startles,
the snail for his hush,
the grasshopper, of insects, for alertness
and his lucky look

End of September

However it may be with me
Lying wakeful in the old bed
This night is cool, fresh, quiet,
Moon-blanched, a few late season crickets
Trill under the oaks across the road,
Some of the moonlight, coming through
The pine tree by the window,
Burns like lumps of phosphorus, on the bedclothes.

Reader Listening

Rain now with dark coming on
after the chill clear day, and it makes
coming against the roof a roof of sound.
Many mild little comments,
with the occasional loud drop,
the faint ones, the pitch
differences, the many drops striking
at almost the same time, the
individual sounds still audible
in the general run of sound as the rain
comes down heavier, loudening
on the roof, the sense of this change
belonging with the sense that comes
when an animal one has been watching—
say a bear, soaking himself in a creek—
suddenly & calmly changes position—
when on the window ledge
a series of drops begins falling,
starting up an excited little
local tempo, and then, oddly, slows down
and at last stops while the heavy rain
continues

… and leaving, then,
for that first companion
of your mere existence (before
you established relations even
with yourself, or your human mother)
the immense brood-beast
the natural universe, where
for instance Homer's 'dark earth
and starry sky and strong-running ocean'
are a corpuscle eddying—
                              not
to be home any more,
with a consciousness like the house
built joist and stud and rafter
in time, in human lengths, not
to pause even at the nestling
of chemical to chemical,
but entering those subtle barrens
where billionths of seconds go,
under the whole show
(leptosome to the last!),
into the sheer and clear
orderliness of chance
where the numbers do their dance
of no location—haunt,
if what I've read is so,
of Heisenberg, and Planck,
and the quiet magister, Gauss

Third Deposition

The lamp throws a pleasant warmth
on the back of the hand, its soft white light
floods shoulder fingers pencil note pad
and desk surface, notes on old soiled scraps of paper,
the Hölderlin, the glasses case, the black bowl
by Blue Corn, the Hokusai Fishermen Draw in Their Nets
While a Poet Meditates in a Distant Hut,
the Porsche ad, The City Porsche, cut out
of an old *Time* years ago, a blue-silver 914
driven by a blonde up a hill in San Francisco,
the 0.5 liter earthenware coffee mug,
the drafts of a poem, "migraine's fancy
stitching" a phrase at the corner of the eye,
piles of old letters—the latest from Helle—
a lucite box of dry flies, clippings of reviews
of books wanted, a lump of turquoise and
a piece of white granite veined with green
from the Snowy Range in Wyoming,
white glue, a pen light disassembled
its batteries exposed, a bit of paper folded so
that a quote from Pope sits up, and crawling across
all this comes the black cat, Christmas, so much
admired by the family, cautiously lowering
and lengthening her body, one glossy paw
testing for a spot to sleep in, settling instead
for the window shelf, hind quarters on a *New York Review*,
front quarters, and cheek, on an old rabbit pelt,
a paw curled over her eyes.

Fragment

... Self
the sly continuator; peevish; writhing
knot of flat-eyed appetites,

no one of which ever notices
the others it's tangled with; old

shapelessness, incessantly bringing on
disorderly assemblies of shapes;

busy attractor of swarms
of gnat-miseries with its sweat; deep

well of pity for its own plights
and tireless accumulator of grievances; inflamed

and swollen with the merit
so gained, with gleeful resentment

concealing its own indestructible
talent for moderate happiness; constantly

aching to be changed into now this
now that icon of calm felicity

Winter Child

Never mind now, I am delighted,
my happiness is complete—
the individual human now recedes
with his motley moderations
on moderate little earth
these days of October,
November, December, when
the mother darkness and cold
come back and the father light
wheels low, aslant, unconcernedly
withdrawn into remoteness,
in the extravagance
he blazes with, and we
come back into the mineral
sleep (a little way) from which
rousing so keenly
in the cold
we see and hear nothing
but the Heart's red fires in the dark, in
the end Silences
where reign the archaic King
and his Queen, that was
before him, in the Beginning.

In the Habitat of the Magpie

Oh, we will get out of here
Where everything's impure, not clear,
Where, as they say, it's all shades of gray,
Won't we, old self (though time I fear
Is getting on…)—like the magpie
We saw springing up today
Lightly from his putrid meal
On the pavement, his feathers
Such a fresh black and white.

Lion Camp

Venus in the darkness of early October
flashes away above the black tip
of the hill behind Lion Camp.
No one else here, so cold.
Taking my old GI blanket I step into the open
and stand wrapped in my own warmth, like a Bedouin
or an Arapaho. Not a sound. No insect,
nighthawk, or owl, the stream so low
it runs without noise
among the dry boulders. I hear my breathing.
What a good garment a blanket was in the old days
for speculative thought, and personal dignity,
arms not free for work, or love, or fighting.
But I've come away with too much
on my mind, and like none of it,
and can only hold it
like a man standing carefully with an armload
so unstable he can't put it down.

The Leaves

Is it the stationariness
of misery that makes it
so bad for the mind?
Motionless over his desk
under the steady brightness
of a small lamp, he hears
with pleasure the wind
in the darkness outside.
Sometimes it thuds on the house.
The house creaks familiarly
as if a big animal had bumped it
casually, in passing. The noise
of the sycamore leaves
rasping across the blacktop
comes in over the hum
of the heater, and some music turned down
on the radio. It is the world
out there, clear of him,
and holding him.
          So: sitting enclosed
by his light, he and his light
by the windy darkness,
with this hangover pain
from a day's work in unwisdom,
what comes to him is no
illumination but, more useful,
a passage from the Journals
of Degas, with its incidental
and modest wisdom: 'The bustle

of things and people takes one's thoughts
off one's troubles. If the leaves
of the trees were motionless
how forlorn the trees would be
and so should we!
There's some kind of tree
in the garden next door that moves
with every breath of wind.'

Demonology

1. Yes, it's distressing, the demon appears in you as quietly
as, say, a large pimple appears overnight on a teenager's nose.
2. In dreams he sometimes resembles a man, sometimes the demons
in old pictures—greenish, a baked-looking skin. He changes rapidly.
3. In your contest with him, you may think at times
to ignore him, having observed that he thrives on attention:
the thought that you have succeeded in this, though,
is a signal to him to come rushing back
with a furiousness that will astound you. You discover he is
more serious than you yourself have ever been.
4. He can, at times, what with the energy and vigilance
he has appropriated in you, almost
acquire the shape and size of a good man.
5. Almost. His weakness is that he can be contained.
He lives inside the life of his host, helping himself
to it generously, and can't surpass his host in magnitude.
When he wins, it's by reducing his host to his own considerable size.
6. He is obstinate. One may take comfort, if one can,
in reflecting that courage is superior to obstinacy.
7. He is mature. No matter what the shape
he takes at the moment, the lines and surfaces are firm.
Observing this, you understand that you are the child
you were, and had better set to learning, as that child learnt.
8. His obstinacy, maturity, energy, ingenuity, and seriousness
enforce a desperation which, for good or ill,
demands action, and there's the whole point. The demon comes
straight from the Nature of Things. His message is simple:
keep moving, you. Hence his own resourcefulness
in suggesting new arrangements, finding opportunities.

9. He cannot be ejected. There's no place to send him. Though Christ
drove some demons into a herd of hogs, and the hogs rushed off
into the sea, into what could he have poured the sea?
Or as Whitehead observed: 'There is no escape from the totality
of the universe, and exclusion is an activity
comparable to inclusion.'
                              So. If the demon can't be
ejected, maybe he can only be made to disappear, right there
within you, as—light from a 40-watt bulb disappears
in light from a 100-watt bulb. Light bulbs? It seemed barren.
Say, then, the way a pool in a dry creek bed
disappears once the creek begins to flow again.
I stopped on that. It was late, a cold wind,
blowing hard since sundown, now was beating
more noisily than ever in the darkness about the house.

NARRATION

During the night a creek came to mind, and a real one,
back in Missouri, outside Columbia, on the hilly
and still half-wooded place owned by a farmer
who let me hunt squirrels there: frost weather,
the clear colors of the hickories and oaks in the still air
startled me every fall when I went back in
where the hunting was best along a creek
with a corn field on one bank which the squirrels
raided in the morning and evening twilights
and along the other bank a wooded rise
where they nested. The creek this time of year
after its spring and summer noise and glitter

was all but dry—its bed silent; clean, round, white
stones, some leaves and dry twigs
lodging between them. The creek wound away from your eye
like a deserted roadway. But at one sharp bend was a pool,
deep and long, crescent-shaped, and clear, despite
the leaves steeping in it that had recently fallen
and now lay stuck to the bottom stones, their colors still fresh:
coming toward that pool once I saw my first kingfisher,
stationed over it on a twig, watching for frogs;
here the squirrels came to drink, leaping over the creek
from the treetops on the opposite slope into the sycamore
that rose beside the pool. Then they spiralled cautiously down,
I sitting there motionless for maybe an hour before one came—
sitting head back, watching the tree where, a hundred feet
up in the air, its huge branches had ample space
between them, its bright leaves, separate, moving a little
now and then in the October air, the high blue dry air;
through the silence would come an occasional miniature crashing
in the deep leaves up the far slope as a squirrel
rushed over the ground from one tree to another
and I waiting, my .22 across my knees,
watching those white, calmly zigzagging upper branches,
and their yellow leaves, hung balanced in that air.
There was no demon there.
The demon, too, was there.

Winslow Homer at Seventy-two

Broken apart in wrinkles, some
the disturbing sort that fork across
the skin without following
facial contours: the eyes
narrowed, heavy-lidded,
looking what seems a hard challenge
down at the camera, but is only the neutral
jolting energy of complete attention
long since involuntary, peremptory and definite
as a bolt of lightning when a branch of it
pokes into a night sky twigs and all, his occupational
affliction and his happiness.

SONNETS FROM *Running at Hendry's*
(*In Plain Air,* 1982)

For head with foot hath private amitie
And both with moons and tides.
—HERBERT

After Work: Foreword

Home, then out of the canyon and inch past
Shopping center, school; inch over freeway;
Veer with the creek that notches the pale clay
Headlands and I am at the place at last.
The shoreline hereabouts runs east and west.
Clear days there's islands to be seen, any day
Sky, sand, waves, light, birds, dogs, people. I'd say
Late in the day in winter is when it's best.
Down the long, slant beach, and the wave-tips catch
The sun's low fire, the wet sand's all red light,
The shorebirds eat red light—and all goes gray
The moment you turn back the other way,
Cliffs, sea, and sky a great cave, in dead light;
And the fresh darkness settling, in the stretch.

Down Here After Being Kept Away
Three Weeks by Sickness

How much I missed this place. While I've been gone
The season has turned, the winter birds are here,
The sand is firm, clean, smooth, and the air clear
With a wave flashing cold in the low sun
Under the slow wingbeats of a pelican
That three pilfering gulls keep swinging near,
Whimbrels and godwits and plovers and killdeer
Work the sleek shallows, I begin to run:
Easy, now. But I swear the beach gives back
My footthuds like the tightly stretched buckskin
It looks like here, the blazing water track
Of the sun's running beside me—coming in
The old ocean commotion and the dark mass
Of a jogging girl's hair jouncing as we pass.

Commotion

Under a low fogbank, the blackish tone
Of its belly darkening the waves and sand
And cliffs that block all view of the high land
Where the town sits in sunlight, I'm alone,
The beach is bare, the hard brown sand slopes down
Steeply to the low tide. From where I stand
No jogger rounds the point to scare the band
Of godwits from their meal. I'll start my run
Together with the dark sea running in
From a horizon turning steely bright
(Sun finishing its run where the fog's thin)
While jaegers and gulls keep up a running fight
Whirling sharp black against that piece of sky
The beach and cliffs run toward and likewise I.

More fog.—Have you seen a gross, heavy-legged deer?
Or in a flight of terns some with the bill
Twisted and blunt, some with stub wings, some small
As wrens? Imagine an ectomorphic bear.
No, shaped by the shapes of water and earth and air
They move in ruthless grace and crucial skill
Unfree and strong and evenly beautiful,
Unprovided with souls, completely clear and here.
I pass a poor old woman, six foot three,
Mannish, who has a heron's jerky stride,
Just as a well-built fellow passes me.
Next, hairy breasts swinging from side to side,
An obese youth rounds the point; and better weather
Brings many another of us out here together.

Running with My Sons

Two of them home by chance the same weekend!
I fight a fear that's like Ben Jonson's fear,
Of being too glad of having them down here
Running abreast with me on the hard smooth sand.
And all the better it is for being unplanned:
I have no heed for shorebirds, or the clear
Sunlight inside the wavelets rippling near,
Or other runners, or the familiar blend
Of surf- and gull-noise.—One of them sprints away
Spattering through the shallows like a pup,
I say to the other "Don't let me hold you up,"
And off he spurts. I watch them happily.
How they shine! across the difference of years,
And will shine in my day fears and night fears.

Running with My Sons

Fifty-one runs with nineteen and twenty-three
Thinking "by hap of happy hap," the phrase
Cast by the crude old Tudor well displays
The kinship of happiness and luck … I see
From the corner of my eye how springily
The boys are striding, how their breathing stays
Easy and light. Not so with them always,
Both once rode crutches after surgery.
We round the second point and they run on
Into the haze, down beach I've never run,
While I turn back, and think of how that stretch
They're running is like the years I'll never reach;
And think helplessly, how will it be for them?
It'll be the same and sharply not the same.

More Hap

Bad omen in the morning and once more
Late in the day, encountering face to face
Two sons of bitches, each at a time and place
I'd never seen either one of them before.
And the day, picketed by this polluting pair,
Went wrong; running in the dusk I now retrace
The slight brain-lurches that put me off my pace …
The slippages of heed that are my despair!
So I run along full of my latest blunder—
And everything's still, but a distant simmering
From the sea, the light rakes low, the tide is neap,
In the strange peace I nearly halt in wonder
At water in thin clear layers wavering
On the flat sand—a kind of shining sleep.

God-light

Low dark cloud-cover and ocean make a pair
Of jaws held just apart; in the opening,
Where I now run, no room for anything
But the cliffs, now bleakly pale where they are bare.
At the horizon, a low, cold light just where
The sun has set; I watch it briefly cling
At the sea's rim—clear God-light, the real thing—
While I run on through suddenly darkening air.
Under the cliffs are sanderlings and plovers
Busy with their last feeding for the day;
And a few people—a lone girl there, two lovers,
An old lady with her dog; and part way
Down the cliff ahead a house hangs, with a flight
Of stairs down to the beach, and window light.

Running Late, Having Held the Class on
Herbert Overtime to Look at Three Lines

Deep dusk, the quarter moon strong enough now
To show in the wave's flank with a fish-like glitter,
I run on the dark beach thinking, This is better
Than the delicate orange clouds two days ago
In pale green sky, too pretty. (Are there no
Other runners here, for once?) Thinking, That wetter
Sand there shines like some membrane, this twitter
Of sleepy sanderlings says it must be so
That I'm the last one out, that subdued roar
Of water's a not-word I have heard before,
And suddenly there comes the one thing more
I ought to have told the class, that not elsewhere
In English is that thought thought—and see how clear
And passionate and quiet it is there.

And the Fat One Gripping
a Bottle of Wine

Blazing November. The wrongness of this weather's what
Makes my being here for anything all wrong, the sea
Having gone slack and pale and bland and summery,
The air since the first light this morning dry and hot
And motionless. Broad day's brought everybody out.
There goes a runner threading through a family
Straggling along in street-clothes. Surfers unseeingly
Step around three elderly ladies. All tramp my holy spot.
I run on sand where multitudes lay and strolled and sat.
It's scuffed and stale. And heading through the overused scene,
Around the last point I see alone out on the flat,
Where the sand's newly wet, one fat girl and one lean
Briefly link arms and dance, whirling this way and that
Over their clear, prancing reflections in the sheen.

Colleague with a Notebook

Beach wide and flat. I run, dully, on a sheet
Of neutral-colored light, slipping along
In the wet is a blurry quarter moon, a tongue
Of water pushes in quietly over the wet,
Quick-sliding, low-hissing, its tip of foamy white
Entering up the sand. Then I'm among
The seal brown, seal high rocks—old seals and young
Seaward they slant, alertly—exposed of late
By the winter tides ... slowly, on the way back,
Darkness coming, the horizon turns a bright,
Deep orange-red, the exact color of the throat
Of a cutthroat trout! Pass a man writing a note
(His camera's set up) and look back—beach black
Where he stands, crossed with great slashes of light.

Loiterer

But the water—a half-inch deep there, sidling in,
Rumpling to sharp little ridges, with elegant
Black shadows, in the level light ... ripplings sent
At an angle through other ripplings cross-hatch, then
The surface quiets, and, smooth once again,
Shivers all over ... two tiny waves, blent
Head-on emerge, each going the way it went ...
New water foams in, slides back clear and thin:
The lovely loiterings, with darkness coming on,
Stay with me as I finish up my run,
Having had to hurry all I did today.
And nothing done well, getting it all done.
"That most exciting perversion," said Hemingway,
Of such forced haste; the feelings fray and splay.

Light Like the Beautiful Trout Fly Name:
Pale Evening Dun

Cold spatter of rain, then wind. Last night the tide
Covering the beach and sliding up the rocks
Along the cliffs, driving the sanderling flocks
And me elsewhere, now a beach five yards wide
All kelp-heaps and scattered stones, and a rock-slide
At the point, wet shale in jagged blocks
Angled for twists, foot-slitherings, bone-shocks;
And pooled and trickling water on every side.
I rock-hop past the next point. Here the air
Is quiet, the ocean crump-crumping its tons
Well out from shore, the nearby water still …
Stretch of smooth sand! with a boulder here and there,
Standing alone—black rock, gray water, duns
Of wet sand, cloud-roofed, in the even light; so beautiful.

Running in the Rain, High Tide

Rain slanting past and no place here to run.
In the cold deepening dusk there comes the roar
Of water much too near; as the car door
Caught by a gust swings wide, I see the brown
Waves smack the cliffs. Well, head for the next beach down.
Bulldozers have gouged it up and gullies pour
With the runoff, crumbling, forcing me to detour
Through garbage to the blacktop (it's near town).
I run in a dazzle of streetlights and car lights
My glasses streaming, and splattering along
Alone, think of the swaggering word invictus;
And sprint back through the drench against a strong
Headwind, wearing as the car comes into sight
A combination grin and runner's rictus.

Running in the Early January Cold

The near water heaves bright gray, then deepening
Outward to a dark horizon line as keen
And aloof as the evenly moving, clean
Crest of a wave, or the edge of a gull's wing:
That pale sunset out there hasn't anything
To do with me, with its cloud whorl, its icy green;
There's nothing in the few people I've seen
To catch the eye, and take away the sting
Of the raw cold look of things; and thinking I run
Upright and briskly, I see my shadow: a tall
Pinhead aslant on stilts, going at a crawl
Along the sand; and in that room today
The neutral silence, I feeling in all I say
The desolateness of what's barely begun.

Willets under an Overcast

This new and winter term is a stopped wheel
To push against, it budges and rolls back
Into its rut in a hard-frozen track
Through the inside country where I think and feel:
Outside the willets land for their evening meal,
Their lifted wings exposing elegant black
And white zigzags, beside the tidal slack:
Gray clouds, gray ocean, and the light still and pale.
Whatever was missing from what I did today
Is the second overcast to run under here,
I puzzle and puzzle under it all the way
To my turn-back place—willets again, a pair
Alight on a black rock offshore, crying *kerlear!*
Teetering prettily, above the sloshing gray.

Big Waves in Wind and Clear Cold Sunlight,
and the Intelligent New Secretary
from the Main Office

Clear from the entrance I could see the spray
Glistening above the cartops like the snow
That banners off the drifts in a big blow,
And once I'm running I watch the falling away
Of waves heaved house-high, and the steady play
Of the cold light on wave-slopes bursting snow
Over the snowy rush and crush below—
Too much for surfers: wave-watchers here today.
And up the beach, a girl sitting quietly
On a big rock, with those waves roaring in.
And it is Marilyn, I recognize
As I come near; sun lights her gold hairpin,
And I start wondering if her blue eyes
Are seeing more than the rest of us down here see.

Old Rocks out in the Late Light

Chill air and the sea sunk, like a lake
In drought-time, back from the gray sand,
A bright place the size of a man's hand
On the waves, where the light comes through a break
In low clouds. And the striped rocks. They take
The eye between flat sea and land,
Humped, leaning, pale band by dark band,
Green-bearded, dripping, with pools that quake
In the raw breeze. Here's one pokes out
At our cliffs a heavy upper jaw
That with the lower grips in its maw
The sand I cross. Surely the brief light
Is holy, and holy the darkness light
Makes when it goes, but not that snout.

A Quiet Fourth

Homesick, building a fly rod on the patio
All the fresh sunny breezy morning; a calm blue
Sky and green leaves close me in. Low tide's at two,
And I'll run then. —The dusty parade and rodeo
Took place in town, all right, forty-five years ago,
A thousand miles away; fireworks afterwards, too,
And then the ride home on the dirt road, winding through
The cool fields in darkness, hearing the water flow
Over the weirs; and then our dogs, at the driveway turn.
—And winter's the time for Hendry's Beach; therefore I'll write
This one, to do for my few summer runs down here:
Beach flat, trampled, sea flat, slack and warm and clear;
People little black figures against the big silver light;
Close up, it's beer can, frisbee, radio, sunburn.

July 4, 1978

A Quiet Fourth

Fran and I much alone this bright mild day
With the boys scattered, friends too, mostly, so
It's Sousa and Ives out on the patio
(And how subtly the Ives lets the attention stray);
Then work on a fly rod, later get away
For a run at Hendry's, when the tide is low.
My last run down there was six weeks ago—
Summer crowds, and a new fee I won't pay.
But on the Fourth you want a crowd, I learn,
So down I go: beach flat, sea calm, clear, warm.
In and beside it, in every tint, size, form,
People, with frisbee, radio, sunburn.
—Drive back, see centered formally on a top stair
A beer, beneath a flag limp in the cooling air.

July 4, 1978

The Other Runner

Recalling, during a drought, a rainy day last year

Wind spread the rain across the glass, I hearing it
While reading Milton all day long, and looking up
From time to time, to wonder when it would stop,
And then forgetting rain, in the warm room where I sat.
Then arriving at the beach: yellow-brown breakers lit
From under a slowly lifting ledge of cloud—the tops
Catching the level blaze, and darkness soon to drop,
And for my run the sand wave-beaten hard and flat.
I ran alone, leaving some saunterers behind,
Beside a set of fresh footprints so far apart
I couldn't match them long, and slowed my pace, resigned;
Thinking of Milton, no, of every excellence,
How it exhilarates and humiliates the heart;
High waves nearing both sets of our footprints.

Dog-days I
Rain-running Recalled

Hard wind, rain; I the only one out here.
Wind on my back, rattle of rain on hat,
Hissing of rain on sand, and beyond that
The noise of the big waves; and small and clear
A whimbrel's call in the din as I draw near
A roaring down the cliff and over the flat
Hard beach—an hour-old river I halt at,
My glasses streaming. The world is a bright smear.
Into a gale now, and the ocean sound
Drowned out by the new howling of the air
Around my head, then even louder pounds
The *hough! hough!* of my lungs inside this blur
Of boisterous air, cliffs, water—startled mind
Along for the ride, body with its old kind.

August 11, 1978

Dog-days II
Incidentally Recalling a Dying Seal

125

—Not that its old kind give a damn for it.
For us who live here, the impersonal
Bright quiet gaze of that dying animal
Put rightly the relation of the fit
And unfit both, to that of which we're knit.
And once the indifference is mutual
Shall consciousness here in the individual
Turn with the whole? the light of light be lit?
I know I saw that seal dying his death
Half sunk into the sand, on the sunny shore
In the tide-wash: with each wave coming in,
The sand sucking him deeper than before,
The water swirling over his head again,
Subsiding, he catching another breath.

Anniversary

Life's uneventful, and while we were gone
The season turned; the winter birds are here
And the crowds gone, and the salt atmosphere
Is sharper, with a low hazed-over sun
Laying its wide and glittery roadway on
Gray ocean that looks lonely. Like last year.
—Over the cliffs two hang-gliders appear,
Slope in and land nearby; I start my run.
Sand smooth, smooth! for a runner or a flyer
In this gray light and chill air's misty blend
And the sanderlings, lively, lovely, never tire,
And the sun suddenly lights a deep red fire
Up on the sand, using a beer can end,
And all of it makes up my heart's desire.

Sanderlings Here

A low fog bank to run inside today,
Wave-noises muffled, near cliffs blurred and pale.
Fog-puffs come down, each spreading a black tail,
A black bill aimed at the sand. And a slight gray
Movement ahead suddenly swerves this way
And a whole flock gleams cleanly purposeful
Against the drifting vapor. Now they all
Vanish up there, sheering themselves away.
And near the finish, a flat stretch, bits of shells
And pebbles lift a little and begin
To travel along the water ahead of me—
Sanderlings, running in the fog or else
Low-gliding, I here running heavily
As faintly they shape unshape and shape again.

Night-piece

Lying in the long dark, insomniac,
I see it clearly: sea and beach and air
And a red winter sun, down low, for fire,
For the fourth element made out by the Greek
On Sicily's coast two dozen centuries back—
Fire that'll turn me into atmosphere
After I'm dead, and ashes tossed out where
Maybe they'll wash ashore. I hear gulls creak,
And put my being in with the elements
We share with the whole show, rather than
With the odd creature in it that is man
Or with my self, still odder ... till the tense
Weavings of wakefulness begin to fray
Loosen and come apart and float away—

... continued

Not bad, for night thoughts, but as Hemingway
Noticed, night thoughts on recollection,
Deep as you went for them, don't pass inspection
Laid out and drying in the light of day.
Something on which there is not much to say,
Sheer Nothingness, once more escapes detection,
Though disciplined minds can reach by indirection
What the imagination hides away ...
Yes, *darkness*, *sundown*, *water*—take your pick
Of pictures: wings, a little boat, dark blue
Of gentians, you can't make any of it stick.
So human, moving, lovely, and untrue.
By the fresh light of morning being bound
To thought that makes the phrase, if not resounding, sound.

The Desolation Light

I came down here one dusk and the beach was gone.
The winter tides were easing it out to sea,
Shelving it down and down, when suddenly
A storm came through and scoured it to the stone—
A jumble of stone; and the sky having done
Its damage loosened up, pale vacancy
Between a lot of ragged cloud debris
Scattering fast, foam yellow and waves brown,
The sea, too, loosened and sprawling, sunk so low
That stubs of rock under for months now showed.
Air darkened as if a curtain had been drawn,
And shining as if for meditating on
Was a tidepool that the gray light had filled
To brimming where a simple stillness held.

News

131

RAVAGED BY NATURE, says the local News,
BEACHES ARE DYING—naturally I read on,
How one day these thin margins will be gone
For good, new sand held back by the dams we use
On our best streams while the sea slowly chews
The old away, back to the cliffs and down
To the stones. And nowhere then to run or sun.
Any dark place can say what else you'll lose:
The canyon air that floats the alder leaf,
The light on the creek, and the creek too, will go;
And the ground under, where it had to flow.
Your sons, and the dear woman who is half your life,
And the two eyes you see both with and through
Will go; and your skeleton; and your spirit, too.

Heron Shapes at Dusk

132

I know the heron that's made this beach his own
Between the headlands, slants like a poised spear
Invisible in the driftwood where I peer—
And there he goes now, flapping off alone.
Later his shape breaks out of some gray stone
That the low tides leave bare this time of year,
Then further down, in deeper dusk, lifts clear
Where only a black tangle of kelp had shown.
Then over by the cliffs, in the near dark there,
I see a heron shape become a girl
Hunched with her trouble there on the driftwood.
The shore a place of human bad and good,
Not herons now, so stony stark her stare
At the late red fading from a cloud-swirl.

Heron Totem

Up the long beach, a flock of sanderlings
Will swoop past a ridge of ocean roaring near
(Their white chests flashing), tilt and disappear,
Or pelicans line up, dark, heavy things,
And form one body with a dozen wings
Approaching me head-on, or godwits flare
Warm cinnamon wing-linings on the gray air
When they veer off in the big flocks winter brings.
I love them all, and most this homely one:
Color of driftwood, among the bustlers, the wary
Swervers, he leans inquiringly, and waits.
Slow, frail, ungainly, set for the long run,
Silent with hope, by nature solitary,
He picks his spot, stands still, and concentrates.

Sunday Run: Starting Out

At the water's edge a baby smacks the beach,
Seriously, then casts me a grave look.
A woman wades along reading a book,
Surf tugging at her legs. And the gulls screech,
And a girl makes a staggering run and reach
For a frisbee through a haze of charcoal smoke
Sharp-scented in the cool air, from a nook
Under the cliffs. We brown and burn and bleach.
And the sober sun, half through the afternoon,
Throws iris-leaf shapes, and squarish glares of light
Along the rollers, sends a quick-sliding thread
Of light along a crest, and overhead
Makes on a softball on its climbing flight
In the blue, a tiny daytime quarter moon.

In Public: *Liberté, Fraternité*

A photographer sets his tripod up and waits
Among various types down here for the sunset;
The unlovely public—whatever it is creates
Us bungles us.... And no colors as yet;
The scuffed-up sand shines gray where it is wet.
The place seems idly jostled, by the gazes
And glances of all these folk, their grunts and phrases.
On the bright gray they bulk in silhouette.

~

And home now, out of the salt atmosphere,
With these things written as I pleased I feel
The doubts crowd in (like a real crowd, watching me
Running along down there), each all too real
And undisguisable deformity
Passing in plain view, in the open here.

What the Sea Muttered

With a variation on a theme of Goya

You haven't kept the reader busy enough.
I know, I know—it comes of my long affair
With the clear and ordinary; all my care
May fail to hold the intensity in the stuff.
Too many off-rhymes, rhythms strained and rough,
You crash the delicate old barrier
Between octave and sestet. I declare
My shame before the masters. *You sheer off*
From the whole truth: not even writing of
That day you found you'd fallen out of love
With running down here, much less of harder themes.
—The reason sleeps, and monsters shape the dreams
Which are the things we're doing in broad day,
The monstrous half-done.... Nolo contendere.

Topophilia

137

Cold dead light, and the beach, from the long rain,
Like a mud-flat under this low cloud-cope; though where
Sun lights the cloud's far edge a pane of clear
Yellow sky joins it to the steady line
Of the horizon; and tiny and black, and fine
In detail, an oil rig sits precisely there
On the skyline, like some miniature
Electronic component, the thin struts showing plain.
And the space out there clear and empty and fine,
Ready for God to fill—like an Inness, a Lane,
Or even a Hopper: and I think of their
Frank and mystical love of light, and plain
Shapes in the great vacancies of air,
And taking comfort in the bare and spare.

Running at Sundown and Dark

Well, it's a pretty sunset—sherbet green,
Orange, even some raspberry, streak the sky
From sea horizon to cliffs. Pelicans ply
The offshore reaches and fishing boats careen
On big waves, giving substance to the scene
With their everyday skillful efforts. Meanwhile I,
Pondering a talk that may well go awry,
Run on the tide-zone's particolored sheen:
Mind pawing obsessively at certain unclear
Distinctions.... Pass two more runners; lovers, one pair;
A lone girl walking slowly back. It's night
When I come in, distinctions still not right,
Past black stumps in the water just off shore—
Surfers, in the dark there, waiting for one more.

FROM *Water Among the Stones*
(1987)

To the heart that has felt it and that is the
true judge, every loss is irretrievable
and every joy indestructible.
— SANTAYANA

I

To My Matilija

Where the canyon walls
Close in, and the air cools,
And the little green trout flick and hover
In the clear green pools
Between the falls
Where that sturdy solitary, the slate-gray dipper, year round, sings
Till the steep stone rings
Is where I'll go, still unforgiving
Of others' and my own poor past
(How keep my mind clear and not curse
Doings that make life worse?)
And be, Matilija, your lover
When I am dead, and at long last
Won't have to make a living.

~

As for the agony
Clenching in me:
My own and others' imperfection,
Killing delight ...
On those clear pools my own reflection
Is broken light.

And in that steep stone cleft
What will be left
Of me is not the middling lover
Here, of a wife
With whom he gladly would live over
A second life—

Nor that one who'd begun
A better son,
Friend, father in his own thinking,
Than he became—
So maimed in the doing (heart here sinking)
And yet the same.

Say all these disappear
Into the sheer
Fire of that anger—what's remaining?
Stranger, the sight,
Say, of the tall slim pale wild oats leaning,
In the late light,

Beautiful, on a stony rise
Before your eyes,
While you stand making out a crossing
Down where the stream
Slips roaring through boulders, and the spray's tossing,
And the alders gleam:

At such a moment, here
I'll stand, tho' not appear
But be coincident with your seeing
The shining scene
And in that moment have my being,
Unhuman, and serene.

II
Festivity

The early morning air at streamside—
    criss-crossed, hung
With an intricate lace, then long
    streamers, of the birdsong
As I tie on a fresh Royal Wulff,
    size 14.

Note: The quotations at the top of the poems are taken from Isaac Walton's
The Compleat Angler, except for the couplet from John Weever above XVI.

III

On a Hillside

There's a movement, and a snake suddenly underfoot
    sliding in the heat, through the dry tangle
Of brown grass and thistles, dead stalks
    of wildflowers. A California Kingsnake it is,
In plain view; he's entering the rock-pile
    beside me, out on his rounds.
The fresh enamel gleam of the close-fitted
    scales unblurred by the dust
He goes upon, his bands of ivory and black,
    crooked-edged, ride motionless
In his gliding. Now, fine-tapered tail-tip quivering
    into thin air, he inches
Himself through a tight bend. Now
    a three-inch section of him shows
At an opening, the bands like box-cars
    travelling past steadily.

IV

Catch and Release

Now the wild trout comes in, tired out—in from the roar
    and splintering light at the falls past the bend
Just upstream—in through the glass-smooth stretch here
    that travels dark green, clear, noiseless, over a great slab
Of sandstone—in toward the black shadow and the dank, sweating
    stone fragments tumbled to the water's edge
Under the cliff.
            He looks transparent as he nears
    my hand, the green ridge of his back
Being exactly the green of the water. Fine and icy,
    hard to the touch, he waits quietly, gills working,
After a last strong slippery lunge, the mist-bow colors
    intimated nicely in the polished steel of his flank.
And my Royal Wulff makes a striking rosette
    in military scarlet, green of peacock, white, cinnamon,
Against the dark shine of his jowl.
            Released now,
    he drifts sideways a bit, hesitant, hovering under
The opened fingers, next to the fast current. Then bolts,
    himself a green smudge above the distinct
Shadow shot downstream, skimming the white bottom sand
    in the sunlight then suddenly accelerating
Toward the scant shade of a young alder standing straight
    on the far bank, thin-branched, its leaves just opening,
A lyrical green light in them; and, back here now,
    on the hands, clean chill scent of trout.

Study of Wild Oats #1

Wild oats agile in the wind
at day's end, along the dusty track
going down-canyon—*Avena
barbata* said the flora, 'common
weed of waste places
and open slopes'—now
frantic in their innocent
agitation, twitch and thrash, now
looking but the more graceful
as they swing violently,
the strong sun of this late evening
burning white through the dried-out
husks that dangle, spaced
evenly in the loose
open panicles, little
shining spearheads, all of them
pointing one way and the whole
shining stand bending lower
under a stiffer wind—they
vibrate, bright rustlers, shy
hissers of early summer
under the brown, still mountain,
its flank filling with shadow—
later on, after nightfall, and
the wind down, their exquisite
shapes standing motionless
unbroken in the clear night.

VI

The Harbinger

You soon drop down to the place,
taking the turn-off, an hour
up-canyon, from the main trail.
Willows and an old, broken alder stand
along the far side of the pool,
above the crossing. Trout lie
out near the middle, now holding beside
the main current, now drifting backward
a foot or so, and, slow-finned, easing
forward again, looking faint
above their shadows; the pool,
with the air quiet, all sleek,
till a dragonfly scrapes it,
or a fish takes a fly wrinkling it.
On the near bank huge boulders
obstruct your way upstream.
There, just this morning, lay
the Alpo can, on its side, new,
empty, clean, on the clean sand
under a shady overhang
of sandstone. What a brisk blare
the orange and blue of the label;
how tight and sure, the fit of the label.

VII

Study of a Baby Rattlesnake

147

The little rattler sleeps on, snug
On the sunlit sandstone boulder, tho' oak shadow
Laps over him now. He has tucked in his head
Near the center of his close coils and folds.

It is getting on toward mid-morning.
His luck still holding, there in the open,
Against a cruising hawk or kingsnake,
He collects the stillness of his boulder, and its warmth,

Into a fine heavy medallion,
In his dark bronze markings.

VIII

At the Concert, After a Day Up There

148

The succession of bright scenes passes through
involuntarily, over this fine old music:
you, Matilija, in the sun, spilling among boulders,
flashing in the shallows, pooled
beside damp shady stone, quick sway of leaves.

IX

Homage to W.C.W.: The Prickly Phlox

The tiny alpine flowers, tundra
blossomers in the Arctic, the wildflowers
of these coast mountains, say
this prickly phlox, this April
in the hard canyon wind
down the Matilija, amid
the drab hugeness and harshness
all around, half frozen, by gravity
gripped and splayed; bitten,
wrinkled and dried by the heat,
whipped by winds, burnt down
to a black stub by wildfire—
look, made small, made
definite, here it roots,
under the brush, in the rocks
with its clean pink petals
arching back, flared from their centers, all
straightforward ardor, distinct
in its requirements and opening out
completely with a delicate fragrance:
intricate and exquisite grave system
of living, in this just-sufficient zone
of indifference where, for now,
the big and little forces,
just balancing, cancel out,

amid which protection
unprotected (the physical universe
being Greek, as under that hard
to make out, fearful 'justice
of Zeus' you find in Homer
or Sophocles)—to feed,
to flower, again and again
to bear and be, in toughness
and delicacy, this strictly
conditional existence, small,
swift, incidental beauty, persisting.

Visit

151

Patch of wet sand there
    by the water's edge
Packed with butterflies
    doing what—drinking?
Till one tottered upward
    to circle me, then others,
One or two at a time,
    and for a moment
I had going around me
    in the playful silence
A big wreath of butterflies,
    that broke away then
And went staggering high
    above the Matilija

XI

Draft from the Matilija

Down off the burnt-off slope
    for a drink, the big snake
Stops me on my way
    home at mid-day
To responsibilities (miles from here
    in what is, for the U.S.,
A well-built little city)—how
    quietly he lies,
In slow, slack curves, broken
    by shadow, among three rocks,
Lowering his chin daintily
    to the Matilija.

~

Having paused to judge of me
    by tonguing the air,
He resumes drinking now,
    letting down and lifting
His U-shaped, thin, flat jaw.
    On and on he drinks, taking
A very little at a time,
    unhurriedly
Slaking the whole length
    of his thirst.

~

Earth's a great harsh gaunt garden
      here, made of spiny chaparral,
And cliffs, bare crests, dry stony slopes,
      the fan that opens, desolate,
Scattered with boulders, below
      this canyon; and, running through,
Narrow, bright and chill among its stones,
      the Matilija.—Born
Somewhere in all this, on his own
      from birth, in the fit
And hard gloss of his scales,
      eye of translucent, dry horn,
Or some clear stone, for his seeing, strange
      but, still, seeing:
He lifts his head at last, done
      with drinking, and without haste
Or hesitation winds out over the water—
      not toward the far bank
But downstream, steering purposefully
      between the rocks, the current
Very fast down there, he lifting his head higher,
      moving rapidly now with an air
Of matter-of-fact eagerness into the loud water
      smashing itself solid white
Among the boulders jammed together
      below, where he vanishes.

~

What is it, to be? Slowly to find yourself
    already alive to some place, alone with
Purposes already forming; what is snake
    intelligence but intelligence
First and last, snake experience
    but wholly experience?
No king of darkness, no god, but something
    as good, I think.... To live,
To live and at midday there, to be
    a snake completely, very thirsty,
And drink your fill, at length, of
    the clear Matilija.

Study of Wild Oats #2: The Fisherman

It is something unhuman in us,
    doubtless (serene,
Though, for what it's worth)
    which now has that figure
Pausing a moment, as if interrupted,
    on a stony rise, to see beside him
A stand of the slender
    wild oats bending
A little stiffly, shivering,
    each long, smooth, hollow
Pale stem filled to the top with late sunlight,
    the husks even brighter, swinging
Under their spikelets, ablaze, in shape like
    narrow fine-pointed lance-heads,
Or, sprung open, bird-bills held wide to call—
    and the creek below them
Splitting to pass between boulders,
    roaring and misting,
The mist carrying away rapidly
    on the up-canyon breezes,
Over the boulders the cold shadows of alders
    beautifully sidling.

John's Lizard

The little lizard waits—slender
    fingers outspread
And long thin whip of a tail
    straight as a ruled line.
Resting quietly on John's palm,
    having been caught
With a looped fiber from a stem
    of grass, he tilts his head now
To hold both John and me in his calm
    direct gaze: entirely
In the moment. Things Florentine goldsmiths
    hammered, enchased, smoothed,
He resembles in elegance; likewise
    the Samurai weapons—stirring and
Practical. By day he hunts and suns, by night
    sleeps undisturbed,
His blanket, his roof, his local government
    the starry universe.

A Leopard Lily

The other flowers are long
    finished, and mix
With the dead weeds and grasses
    on the slopes, in the gullies,
Among the rocks. So for you,
    leopard lily—
Tired as we are, late
    in the long day—
We leave the trail, cross
    through the charred brush
To see you: against
    the black hillside
Sending your tall stem
    straight up, your five
Great bright flowers tilted
    at various angles
Way out from the stem
    like bells swinging,
Not knowing—or maybe knowing—
    the festivities are over.

XV

In Late March Up There

Under the hillside ceanothus
    in pale bloom, blooms
A nightshade, bright fresh blue
    in shadow. Here below,
Sits a tiny stone-colored frog,
    looking very knowing in his stone niche …
Bitter scent of skunk on the wind, ahead
    old tortoise on poolside rock
Head and neck outstretched,
    sunning his throat.
And the fishing's in low, clear water
    the sun pouring straight down,
And scarce cover, just the shelving
    shale and the boulders,
The set of difficulties
    slightly different
At every run and pool. Working
    upstream, a happiness near complete,
Among such quick-to-declare-themselves
    factualities.

XVI

The End of Something

I have come here late in the day.
    Now the light is failing, and
What I've just seen's the dead
    gleam of aluminum,
The shape of something, across
    a half mile of chaparral,
Up near the lovely pool
    where the snake was drinking.
When the end of something comes, often
    the signal is ironically
Slight. Goodbye Matilija.
    By the time I reach it—
It's a house trailer, laundry
    flying on a line
Strung on the low bluff
    above the pool—
I have passed two others,
    assorted bulldozers,
Dump trucks, trench-diggers....
    Nothing is ours,
Matilija, I well know.
    How often though

Through how many years—but
      time to go: to
Go and pack out with me
      my useless grief,
Of which neither this place,
      which I know I've loved
Too much, nor any other,
      will bear a trace.

XVII

Yucca whipplei

This big capsule
I plucked green
reaching high
along the stalk
late this spring,
and week by week
let it brown,
and wither, and crack.
Pick it up
and shake it now—
Cha cha it
whispers here
in my study
Cha cha
Cha. Faithful,
dry, and shy
sound of the promise
of *Yucca whipplei*,
calm presence
sending high,
out of its fierce
tipped-with-spines
rosette of blades,
that stout stem
tapering green
above boulders,
in dry gulches,
in strong sun

on stony slopes,
breaking out
its white blossoms,
a great cone of them,
curled and tumbled,
where, in the quivering
heat the light
comes in and is creamy,
cool and still; where
the mind can go
when it wants to.

~

… and a low wind in the alder grove —
or is it the little waterfall? —
mutters from ancient Isaiah thus:
Thou hast multiplied the nation
and not increased the joy.

~

*All stories, if continued far enough, end in death, and he is no
true-story teller who would keep that from you.*
— HEMINGWAY

ON THE NORTH FORK

Dream Vision

Well, it's an old affair—
Stronger than ever, though,
This twenty-seventh year
That I've been coming here.
The memory stays clear
How other places, too,
Brought transient happiness;
I was just passing through
And therefore could avoid
Seeing them destroyed.
But much the same is so
Matilija, with you
As from the first I knew:
I have been passing through—
The difference being, here
Your ruin, though delayed
A bit will be, I guess,
The one I'll stay and bear.

~

At the ranch headquarters, which
you have to walk through
to get up here, an old
yellow Lab with flabby,
drawn-down dugs and, this past
year or so, a bad shoulder,
stands waiting to greet me, in
her usual quiet good humor.
I am an old admirer.
Last year she'd still join us,
lame as she was then,
to fetch the sticks she'd have
one or another of us fling
again and again into
the icy currents.
            She can just bear
the pain it costs her now
to take a step. As I push on,
she stands there a bit, before
making her way back to the porch.
Her eyes half close with the pleasure
from our meeting, her tail wagging
just a little, reminiscently.
Still the enthusiast; while
in her whole manner you see
her unreluctant recognition of
the scope left to her now, including
the clear if receding view
of how, with her, things used to be.

~

Over and over the gods
Fail what they came to guard;
Yours too, poor little stream,
With your lower crossings all
Dry stones, bulldozer-scarred;
Slammed through by mountain bikes
I wonder what god likes,
That's now having his day
(Sees 'em come slashing down
At top speed on their way
To get trucked back to town),
All your bright-bodied trout,
In your shrunk pools, jerked out
By jerks with spinning rods ...
Well well, let me be fair,
The herons took their share.

~

The upper gorge: rest stop,
Midday; and half asleep
I hear your waterfall,
Maybe six inches tall,
Through alder and foothill ash
Gurgle hiss glug and splash
Between your banks and steep
Clean sandstone, that goes up,
Up to the yucca, small
With distance, along the top.

A coolness on my face
Breathes from the whole place—
Your remnant song, that seems
Reflective, now, subdued,
Sounding entirely good.

~

With such things on my chest,
And with my Thermarest
Between me and the stones
And sticks, to spare old bones
That have no flesh to spare—
Outstretched, with eyes covered
Beside this upper reach,
With your much dwindled stream
Still making itself heard
I went down into sleep
Through the leaf-shady air.
In my sleep came a dream,
And in the dream (I swear)
A vision, then a speech,
Abrupt as a sonic boom,
That broke into the hush
I faced in a long room
In which I used to teach—
Broke, then went on in a rush,
In which the vision hovered.
Here it is, word for word:

Our little earth's a goner—
As anyone can see
With or without a book,
You only need to look—
The whole revolting disaster
Being inflicted on her
North south east and west
Now uncontrollably
Coming straight at us faster
Than anybody guessed.
Once and for all, right here,
Come drop with me, a tear
For her, as dwelling-place
For us, the one earth-race
That hasn't belonged here
From the outset: the ones
Whose hearts have been elsewhere,
In this or that Elphame
I won't take time to name;
Neither would I seek
To parcel out the blame:
By nature, so to speak,
We are space aliens.
The space, between our ears.
How lately we have known
That we are on our own.

And after we are gone?
(Be sure that we'll be gone.)
Well, after we are gone,

If anyone should care,
So goes one prophecy
Fitting in its grandeur,
And true, for all of me—
A various multitude
Of the bacteria
Will rule the biosphere,
Their center everywhere,
Humble inheritors
Guarding the true and good;
And all we've understood
Of all that has most mattered,
And, understood, have spoken
In music, paint, words, stone,
In number, and the rest
Till it all stood complete
As nearly as could be—
And perishable, though
After each overthrow
Learned all over again
And more still—all this broken
In ultimate defeat,
The litter of it scattered
On earth *that spinning sleeps*
On her soft axle, while
She paces even, and bears
Thee soft with the smooth air
Along (that's as she crossed
Our gaze in *Paradise Lost*)....

For us, though, let's not grieve—
Nor turn in treachery
On our own kind, at heart
Finding life hard to leave,
Finding it sweet to be
Even if in prospect
Only, for the most part,
As certain sages claim,
And likely to be wrecked.
And deeply as fear goes,
Having in view a good
That, clearly understood,
Comes always at great cost
And always incomplete
And sooner or later lost;
Even so, to repeat,
Our being remains sweet
Under the deepest fears,
In human hardihood.

The vision paused, then said,

Last night I heard a song
Coming through leafy air—
Though fading before long
It sings on in my head:

The earth that once made us,
Being the same earth that made
The dragonfly, the deer,

Lizard and mastodon,
Worm, leaf, stone, bright green blade,
Hill, river, and so on—
When we, in what we do
Ravage it all—this, too,
Is a natural result
For us, the boldest one
Of all her experiments;
In which to fail, long since
We've learned is not a fault.
Experiments mostly fail.
Ours had a good long run.

"Many the wonders," so
Sophocles long ago
Remarked, "and of them none
To match us."
                    Let that be
(With ambiguity
Worked in by history)
Of all that we can see
Of what, now, we have done,
The thing to reflect on.

Just so the voice-vision spoke,
And cold and stiff I woke.
Whether the dream was so
I'm not the one to know.

~

Pretty tired coming back down
today, too. Birds are difficult
to identify against this light.
Sudden black shapes bank and vanish,
light flashing, uncolored, off a wing,
a glossy back. Meanwhile just ahead
beside the trail the little sycamore
with its as yet entire and at the moment
motionless set of yellow and bronze leaves
has lit up like a lamp, backed by
the cold shadow of the great ridge
where the sun just now touched down.

~

 The whole day I've been alone.
 And now I see a woman
 a fair distance away,
 standing just off the trail,
 and looking up intently
 into the dark treetops,
 quite unaware of me
 under my big daypack
 approaching through the dusk.

 Since she still hasn't moved
 I click my walking staff
 against a trailside rock
 letting her know I'm here
 before I come too near

and perhaps startle her.
She gives me the briefest glance
and goes back to her gazing
and soon I am drawing near her.
She is a tall, plump woman,
well into middle age,
dressed in T-shirt and jeans,
looking as if she'd just
stepped outside the house:
no hat, no jacket, no
binoculars, no daypack;
up here alone, it seems,
maintaining this rapt stillness
in the stillness, as the birds stir
high up in the foliage,
darkness a half hour off,
the canyon chill increasing.
"There's a lot of birds up here,"
she says, an eagerness showing
a little, and a slight shyness,
under the factual manner.
I nod and mention seeing
some signs of bear up above.
She rounds our meeting off,
"We saw bears on Pine Mountain,"
releasing us to resume
the solitudes we broke,
she mine, that is, I hers.
I go and she stays on.
I meet nobody else

The rest of the way down.
The appearances all say
she has come up here alone
and on the spur of the moment.
It is dark when I reach my car.

After-words

Each of us varyingly
Has come here from the ocean,
And once here each waits
On a set of varied fates
Now and then not kindly. Still,
Despite my streamside vision,
I've left off sermonizing.
The frayed old pack I carry
Back down this long-loved trail
Contains no remedy.

My spirits have stayed high.
If asked for a reason why
I'd use this mystery
In indirect reply:
The blinded Samurai
Taira no Tomoume
In Yoshitoshi's print
Declines to stand apart,
Fights in the thick of it
Bearing, as talisman,
A poem-slip, that says
Even in darkness, one
Can see the moon with the heart.
But there's no moon in this print,
No indirect sign of it,
In shadow, or weapon-glint,
For us with eyes, to see.
(It is this print alone

which is without a moon.)
Say Yoshitoshi meant
To say a no-moon is
An aspect of the moon
Which he cannot omit,
That once, there was no moon,
And that there'll be no moon
Again, in time; that these
Twinned non-existences
Accompany the moon,
It never goes alone;
Which a blind Samurai
Found with his darkness-eyes,
Leaving him battle-fit
On ground two no-moons lit.

Note: The print is number 33 in Yoshitoshi's *One Hundred Aspects of the Moon.*

And let thine own times as an old story be.
—DONNE

These too, for Fran —

Poems are not what you head for
When we go into a bookstore.
Handed these, maybe you'll recall
How, without fail, when they were small
The boys brought home their dinosaurs
(The long flanks brightened up with flowers),
Houses with slanting chimneys, trees
Of course, a dog complete with fleas …
We taped them to the walls and doors
So you will understand with these,
The bringing of them makes them yours.

Martial of Bilbilis

178

Nothing in Rome escaped his glance, he understood
    This touchy sort of verse,
   And mixed the poor ones with the good:
   Your even book, he said, is worse.

Old and fed up this son of Bilbilis went home,
    A harsh hill town with a cold
   River below, that shipped to Rome
   A lot of iron, a little gold.

Old Man Afraid

Whiskey of youth once mine,
White fire straight from the coil
    Of a hidden still ...
Cool, dark I keep the wine
Of age, that yet may spoil,
    Or handled, spill.

The Morning of Glenn Gould's Funeral

Hearing him now on the car stereo—
    That's as he wished it when alive—
    I look for browsing deer, and slow
    For the tight down-curves as I drive
      Through deep oak shadows
    Over the back way to Ojai.
The October day burns quiet bright and dry
      In the brown meadows.

The thing he's playing's a rocky-riffled clear
    Mountain stream of a piece by Bach:
    The bright quick-moving length of it's here
    Along with sun and oak and rock
      O brief survival
    Glittering in the light and air
And in the dark unbreakable silence there
      The new arrival.

The Two Fields, Where I Used to Live

Nothing lasts, and … in that very fact lies some of
its glory; the sadness … is really not so terrible.
—ISAK DINESEN

Where each oat tassel turns
    in its own air
On its own white fiber
    well out from the stem—
And the barley beards out, rasping
    the fingertips,
Both oats and barley bending
    bright metal they made
Of brightness, dryness, heat
    in authoritative silence—
The fields two shining rectangles,
    below them, black there
In the tangle of rough grasses
    at the fields' end,
The shade of the big glisteners,
    cottonwoods that found
The little stream underground
    before it rises
Where the three fences meet, where
    the gully opens,
Where in the quiet the redwings
    sway the cattails:
Small grain fields of our high country
    with the cold mountains lifting
Above you the crooked line
    of their crests!
The whole scene nears and clears
    now, across fifty years—

Though now, where the great trees grew,
    now, where the stream came up
Whirling a little bright sand,
    the traffic vrooms—
Though the houses of strangers stand
    where the grain bent,
With its own innocence and
    wisdom implicit—
The whole scene nears and clears
    now, across fifty years.

Geron at 3:00 A.M.

183

August, a full moon.
Avoid that window. The lawn
Is cold white marble.

Geron the Heron

A fragment

184

> There, leaning alone,
> A thin crooked dark shape inside the blaze
> Of the low sun and the blaze-back of the sea:
> Now the breeze freshens, lifting his scant crest. He
> Is finishing this one more of certain days
> He has made his own.

Sophocles: *Antigone 332–372*

There is much that's wondrous, much that awakens dread—
Nothing more so than the human, *Sophocles says,*
In the best description of us ever made:
This creature crosses the gray sea in the winter
With the storm-winds, making his way along
In the troughs of the billows,
And of all goddesses the one greatest, Earth
The undying, the tireless—he wears her down
With his plowing back and forth, year after year.

The light-witted race of the birds he takes,
And the tribes of the wild beasts, and the swimmers
Through sea-deeps, in the meshy folds of his nets,
This busy-thinking human.
With his tactics he masters the field-dwellers,
And the hill-ranging animals; shaggy-maned
Horses he reins in, he yokes the necks
Of the powerful bulls he brings down from the mountains.

And speech, and wind-quick thought, and living
In a city together, he taught himself, and how to avoid
The bolts of storms, and having to sleep out
In cold clear weather. He is all inventiveness.
Never does he go bereft of means into
The future. Death alone he cannot contrive to elude; though
From hopeless diseases he has found escapes.

Cleverness surpassing all hopes he possesses
In his plans and devices; by which sometimes to evil
Sometimes to excellence he creeps. Honoring

Earth and her laws, and the sworn justice
Of the gods, he may thrive in his city.—Shun him
When he harms what's good out of recklessness,
Shun the contagion of an arrogant cast of mind....

In Sleep in the Early Morning

… I had begun hearing
a voice that was mine
blent with another's
both unknown and familiar
as it said matter-of-factly
'… have a cup of coffee
with God,' and I sat down
at the bare wood table
in the tiny and quiet
odd-angled café
while Vincent van Gogh
drew up a chair
across from me, God
there inside him,
I saw from the outset,
there and nowhere else.

And though it ended
with both a strong voice
and a text in Perpetua
saying 'God exists. God exists.'
(and of course me impressed,
though I'm no believer)
the great thing was
how van Gogh and I
were both leaning forward

for some unhurried talk
over coffee on how,
in the exigencies (as we found,
they're unpitying, changeless)
of these most ancient arts,
paintings can be painted
today, poems written.

Fran

a fragment

189

In company, in taking pleasure, quite without fuss,
    And zestful, and at once alone,
    At least apart, and here with us,
    She knows that nothing is our own,
        Is almost shy
    In a quiet personal to her
With room for other thoughts to occur.
        Her spirits, high,

No timid moderation there! And yet not bitten
    By this desire and that, like me
    Who goes through life being smitten …
    How her laughter comes out free
        Racy and full—
    Though good comes compact with bad
And justice from the gods is baffling, sad,
        Or terrible.

Reality doesn't last very long.
—SIMENON

Long Shadow Instants at Hendry's Beach

The sun is going down over the slack
Pale surface of a sea at minus tide.
It is large and its light is rich.

Streaming across the water, it
Picks out in bright jags
The crust-like foam which rims
Low-lapping crests easing shoreward.

Onshore the light is soaking into the white, soft-looking
Fur of the flank of a black-lipped Samoyed
Which is standing there quietly. The light is shaping
Itself to perfection onto the contours of
The strong legs of the girl who owns the dog.

She's in shorts and sweatshirt; idly
Dabbles her toes in the thin ripplings
Of the backwash; head down, mind elsewhere. The light
Smooths itself with a finishing intensity
Over the figure of a crippled girl:
She is laughing politely while she shrinks

(But just perceptibly) from an Irish setter
Which has just come dashing madly up to her
While its owner, a thin little girl
Of perhaps seven, mortified, is frantically
Calling out to her 'She likes you!'

And hurrying forward.... *All of it equally
In this lovely, momentary light,* thinks a bent old man
Taking it in, who just then, with a start
At the unlikeliness of it, separately

Becomes aware that he has been feeling
Like a boy this whole day. *Which has not happened
Before,* he reflects. *Wouldn't expect it to again.*

Late December, 1992

'For the life of a man comes upon him
slowly and insensibly ...'
—*Jeremy Taylor*

He puts down his book — it is
the works of one of the number of
the old poets he still loves very much, has
loved for a long time — and noticing
the loveliness of the weak light
of the winter afternoon sloping in
and lying so bleakly and hesitantly
and quietly on the rounded upper
surfaces of the bare branches
and knobby twigs of the trees
he can see from the window,
he thinks, *And that, just as
it is just now — that is plenty.*

The Watch Dog

The terrier barks. I look up from reading and find
the afternoon is over. Voices—some people going by, their
movements just detectable through the high hedge. They are
out for a walk on this first spring-like evening of the year.
The terrier stays tensed—ears forward, she keeps watching
on hind legs at the window. She barks again—two sharp
hard barks, for good measure. The light is mild
on the new green already flecking the old, stubborn dark of
the oaks crowding together up the steep slope opposite,
mild on our apple tree divided by window squares, its thin
crossing twigs still bent from last year, still bare. The street
is quiet again along its length, moments are all we have.

An early spring day on
the upper Santa Ynez, exploring, doing a little
fishing, bringing in his daypack, along with
trout-flies and lunch, the paperback
Greek Anthology made
by Peter Jay

Here were no noises of high-up water
dropping over rock ledges, nor had herders,
in the first big storms last fall, left behind
propped against trees their roughed-in
woodcarvings of the girls of groves, nor were there
young women in cut stone standing under the falls,
smooth beneath their thin dresses of the
creasing water; nor was there any tablet left here,
by a late-summer traveller, in thanks
for the shade and grass and running water.
He had leaned his fly-rod in the fork
of a weedstalk gray from a year
of the weather, and sat reading
Leonidas, and eating a sandwich. Below him   The gods
sprawled the remains of an enormous oak,   of the Greeks
long fallen, the underparts softening   long gone, the
into dirt. The chill green fire of   nature of things
the week-old grass worked into them, and on   from which they
downslope to the little river running clear   arose is as
in sunlight. A pair of young oaks nearby   it was and
checked a cold wind. He was alone   will always be.
the whole day in that backcountry. Once
he put the book down to rest his eyes on

the two oaks. They would move only slightly,
briefly, in the gusts. Fresh in their strength,
crisp, pitiless, splendid from stem outward
to their clear leaf-limits, hard trunks
stone smooth, stone colored, they were OK
as the small deities of this steep place.

Manzana Cow and Dragonflies

—there was a red lizard, brick
red—and a red cow in the creek,
showing through the willows, sloshing
awkwardly upstream bawling
frantically for her calf,
which she had lost somehow.

Diving from overhead
came skipping across the pool
where I had caught the rainbow
two dragonflies—Chinese red.
Then an electric blue
dragonfly shot by too.

Then finest of all came one
(Christ! this was years ago)
the color of the air.
I could best see her where
she floated on the stone
in shadow-duplicate,

distinct where she was not;
seeming, herself, almost
her own faint-featured ghost
over her charcoal show
of self on things below;
and free of anguish there.

1982, 1992

Fall in Spring
(Blue Canyon)

During that time he was nearing
the far side of his own autumn,
with its grants of a certain number
of clear, still days, with a fugitive
richness of colors against the dusks
coming early across chilly ground.
And in that place, on that day, wondering
if there were trout back up in there,
he had caught a small one in the pool
above a crossing, and letting him go
stood for a moment, looking at the pebbles
in their different colors, in the shallows there,
thinking—not sadly, but as the outcome of a rough
calculation—This may be the last time
I'll be up here, and do this. And so it was,
on that shady feeder stream, in that steep place.
He recalls how the road down to it had turned
to a little mountain stream, along a stretch
where the water had shifted its bed in a storm;
that he saw some Mountain Bluebirds in migration.

1983, 1991

A recent spur-of-the-moment hike into
the back-country on the watershed
just to the south

In this fifth year of drought
the Poison Oak has turned
the scarlet of October in
mid-June—an early quitter.
Before noon feeling worn out—
hot and out of breath, glasses
sweaty, up here with scant water and
no food, he was resting on a shady
boulder out in mid-stream.
The little stream had led him on.
He had not thought he would
go so far up in. Dry
through much of its course,
here the Matilija still
ran—slow, low, clear. (And
not potable.) Through the heat-tremors,
high on the stony slope, in full sun,
a scattering of that early scarlet showed,
in with a stand of the satiny white
flower-like dried bracts
of the California Ever-
lasting. It made a fine mock
wildflower stand astir
in the quivery glare
and gusts of baking air—dry air
streaked with faintest tangs
(was he imagining this?) off
the chaparral, off Yarrow,
off the bitter and the minty

herbs, the occasional rank
sunflower, the six different sages,
the streamside Bays, the Yerba
Santa, that tastes bitter at first,
later on, cool; all the while, from
upstream and down there came
the different water sounds
over various distances, changing
with the swerves of the light wind,
the occasional gusts. This was one
of the times when the more carefully
you listen to the water, the less
you can tell whether it's partly voices
of hikers approaching upstream
or down, blent over the middle
distances, varying in pitch,
in loudness—or is nothing but noises
of the water going fast
through the shallows, or slipping
over low sandstone ledges, or pooled
behind jammed boulders and splitting
into narrow falls—sounds
filtering through the shadowy Alders
and Bays, mixed in with their rustlings,
carried by the air currents
over water currents, or glancing
off the damp stone of a cliff, in
the near day-long shadow and coolness
of the narrows not too far up from here.

from A Few Aspects of the Moon

Dusk—city and harbor lighting up below—how
quickly the Mission grounds become all
but deserted. She wanted us up here tonight
to see the full moon rise, having suddenly
recalled such a visit many Octobers ago. And these
others, left over from the day here?—The two
young Latinas idling, idling in silence
by the lavanderia? That young male lurking
(what for?) by the big arch? The middle-aged
bald businessman up on the colonnade, pacing
slowly back and forth, in shirtsleeves,
head down, puffing hard on his stub of a cigar?

'There it is,' she says. Immediately the young man
slips out of the tree-dark behind us for
a look. It is switched-on stadium lights
down by the beach, behind some trees

and this wait's tedious. We go for a walk.
The moon edges up from trees on a hill
and as we pause someone behind us says
'It's beautiful, isn't it,' and
stops beside us to add, 'We used to watch it
from the back porch.' An old man, he crosses his grass
to his car, we round the corner, head down the street
—she looking over her shoulder, for the back porch.

How fine if Tsukioka Yoshi-
toshi could be standing here this dawn
at the window to see the white moon hanging
a little while from the white limb
high in the sycamore and the big flicker black
in silhouette against it, clinging to
a thin, jointed, sharply-bent-down twig
and jabbing the whole length of his bill into one
of our hundreds of prime, dead-ripe persimmons.

Going to Pine Mountain again!
after many years, and just because yesterday
a friend spoke of his own recent visit.
The moon will rise and entangle
itself in the huge old pines up there; and
when that happens—I'll be exactly where?

One for the laments our time begets:
where I grew up the October moon
used to rise huge from behind
the Arms boys' paintless barn with its gambrel
roof and rooster vane, on the round hill
across the draw two farms away—
fit for a thirties postcard photograph.
Both Arms boys are dead. The barn got torn down
and its weather-silvered boards hauled off for use
in bars, barbecue joints and such—as for
the round hill—the 'dozers flattened it
for fill. What the moon rises on over there
tonight is not worth glancing toward.

Out to mail a letter
and there it is—
the midmorning moon which
Stravinsky in his last year
of life, after surgery,
said he was pale as
(a glass of champagne
left standing overnight
was the air the day
Stravinsky died,
the sparkle gone).

At 3:00 A.M. out of bed
with a belly-ache, see
no moon, only how dead
white are the red
bricks of the entry, how black
a roof-post shadow can be.

Darkness comes on. My 65th
birthday nears in the dark
of the year, dark of the moon
too: dark I have never feared,
but liked even when small; *e.g.*
getting warm under heavy
covers in the icy room,
sure of the coming on
of sleep, as I lay alone
in the familiar silent dark
upstairs. —Truth is, with you
though, moon, I can get into
difficulties: have sometimes a
nagging unease at finding
myself in your presence, have felt
more than once terror
at your full white face, can
be resentful at the
thought of your thin light
diluting the dark; dark
that Homer called the holy dark.

I lie awake in the small hours
and think how in the heatless
mind-light of a dream I never see
a shadow. Very pale shadows
of the old pine tree are moving
hesitantly, back and forth,
in the folds of the thin curtains, and
it is a half moon in the clear night.

Well, moon, enough of these
that your Yoshitoshi, who left us
a hundred moon-prints, started
me up on. You don't mesh with our
calendar or clock, or day
or month or year, you claim
your own month—*mooneth*—with its
bunch of ill-fitting moon
numbers, 29 (days), 12 (hours),
44 (minutes), and tonight you are
complete, O smooth one, and in
that matchless silence you
command, how you keep
perfect now at your maximum
brightness that delicate, clean rim,
as of what metal, hammered thin?

from
With a Half Hour to Revisit Yoshitoshi's *One Hundred Aspects of the Moon* at the Museum

The general is seated
cross-legged beside the lamp
in the closed-off inner room,
on his knee rests the hand
gripping his suicide knife,
the just unsheathed blade
upright. Under his gaze,
on the floor, lies the poem
he has finished. It speaks of his
part in a disastrous defeat.
The tiger's head on the wall,
a great strip of shaggy pelt
looped around its neck and
hanging to the floor, glares off
above and past the seated man.
—Where, however, is the moon? Look,
the moon is in his poem.

    It is a summer moon.

The two scholars with their oarsman
have anchored under the Red Cliffs.
A little moon lights up the water
from a great distance, the water
is rippling, the cliffs lean
among themselves. The scholars wait.
Eight hundred years before them
Su Tung-p'o, coming here with friends,
wrote of the cliffs, the
little moon so distant, the lit water.
The scholars wait—for the way to be in
the presence of the moon, and water, and cliffs,
in that full understanding
possessed by Su Tung-p'o.

Stillness of evening: Murasaki
is sitting chin in hand
at the writing desk, set up
for her on a balcony of
the temple retreat; above her
a lantern glows, suspended
from an unseen roof-timber
over the railing; and blocked
in part by the lantern, shines
the full moon: a line-up
of three lights—Murasaki
being the greatest of these—while
everywhere both visible and hidden burns
the fourth light Yoshitoshi.

The White Boat

To close out the year

Light fading and the marsh
Wide now with the tide out,
Darkening, sky pale, bright
Patches of water near,
Bright streaks of it far off
Over the flats. Bird-cries

Cross the stillness: black shapes
On the water-shine,
Willet, Whimbrel, Godwit,
Feeding in a hurry,
Much back-and-forth movement,
Quarrel-cries. Curved bills, wings

Clear on the after-glow,
Curlews glide in. Chitter
Of a Kingfisher: low
Whir over the water
Shoreward, to a dark tree.
Heron, dusk-blue in dusk

Where the sandy path bends
By the marsh-edge, listens
Dead still in mid-stride.
Air ripples the distance,
Small boats drift, fishermen
Hunched on the water-blaze.

Sky over the spit's gone
Smoky red now; low lights
Along the north bay, more

On hills across the marsh
Jump, air-jostled. A last
Puff of warm land air dies.

~

From the boat basin now
Through the late dusk the white
Rowboat comes sliding out
On the still water, white
Reflection under it
Slides along upside down.

Oarsman's figure just
Visible through the dusk
Moving off rapidly
In the silence, without
Noise of splash or creaking,
A good hand at the oars.

Night Heron flies over,
Squawks once, the marsh is dark
Inlaid with thin pale strips,
Oarsman rounding the point
Now heads up bay and boards
A sailboat at anchor.

Breeze now, the bay glimmers,
And that oarsman's in fact
A girl, her silhouette
Miniature in distance;

Wearing a dress, her long
Hair and long skirt blowing—

She sets out to work on deck
Without delay, bending
This way and that, cranking,
Lifting, rearranging—
Every movement practiced
And quick and unhurried.

Then the girl goes below,
Is all; her disappearance
As brisk as her other
Doings. The boat rocks, stays
Dark on the bay's paleness.
Then light at a porthole.

Night nears now, fishermen
Heading in, clear voices
Come small over the flats,
Birds settling in, restless
Bustlings, creaky cries, some
Still feeding in tide pools.

The fishermen arriving
Cut their motor and coast
On the quiet water
Of the small-boat basin,
Through the dark a man's voice
Sounds close in the stillness.

~

This is how it is here
And will and will not be
Again, these small doings
Each an end, a beginning,
A middle, overlapping
Momently, here only,

This year, and then next year
Again, especial, late
In the day then, in late
December, this is how
It will be, and not be.
How it is here.

Morro Bay
December 19, 1979; 1992

‘Is the Universe Trivial?’

(Title of forthcoming lecture by physicist up here from Cal Tech)

And is the answer ‘Yes’?
I have a hunch it is.
I know I’d leave the hall
Uncomfortably full
Of mathematical
High-powered subtleties
I couldn’t even guess
The strangeness of, much less
The forces that they show
Held in their symbol-net;
So I’m not going to go.
I have a hunch it is,
Though; having lived in it
For sixty and more years
And heard the news one hears
From the astronomers,
Of bent space going on
And on and on and on
Before you’ve well begun
To drift much past the sun;
Where, for people at their lives,
Roads and rivers and trees,
Bookstores, gardens, cafes
And theaters, and baseball,
Music, and pictures, all
You get’s dark vacancies
And silence going by
With your occasional
Physico-chemical
Huge whirler hurtling through

Their remoter distances
(Airless, and what is more
Too cold or hot for you)—
Urania declares
That if your ship arrives
You'll be freeze-dried, or burned
Precipitantly away—
There's inconceivable
Violence ashore.

—I have a hunch it is,
So far as we're concerned,
Until it comes to us:
We hold it in our heads,
We featherless bipeds.
—Where it alone begins
Is where the meaning thins:
A horror, truth to tell.
Here's paradise, there's hell:
Oh yes, it's trivial—
Apart from the not-so-small
And inescapable
Fact that it has us all
        By the short hairs.

Ballad of the Subfusc Day

Gray inside, and the overcast
    Outside is staying put
When I get down to it at last
    Doors and windows shut.

But words don't crowd in now, the way
    They did last week for me—
Gave them some shoves and there they lay
    Fitted like tesserae.

Silence. I probe with a broomstraw
    Inside a lampshade pleat
An odd shadow I just saw:
    An earwig lands on his feet.

Oily and slim, he trots along
    My desktop, hunting a crack;
I place him where earwigs belong,
    Between two bricks out back.

More silence. I get up and gaze
    At the woodpile and pine tree
Thinking of certain sunny days
    And wishing I might see

The big Fox Sparrow, say—the one
    Last year who came and went,
His sides and back rainy-earth brown
    And a magnificent

Central chest spot, irregular
        And bold—as for his song,
He was a rich, clear whistler.
        Nothing in him not strong.

What did I see out there instead
        But a rat—a young one, shy,
Intelligent—almost, as my wife said,
        Pretty, in silvery gray.

He matched a silvery stick of pine
        I'd left there, at the tip
Of which he paused, working his fine-
        ly whiskered upper lip:

The first rat here we ever saw.
        And we two stood entranced
Watching him daintily withdraw.
        And the dull day advanced.

And inside, in the same gray air
        Alone once more, I sat
And made place for that seemly pair
        The earwig and the rat.

Fragment on a Theme by Ausonius

Remembering early fall evenings on the Upper North Fork, Matilija

… now that the evening star is bringing on
earlier the day's last light and its shadows,
how many minutes more will that calm reach
hold the bright tan hillside? and the dark bay leaves
make dark bay leaves on the surface along the bank
of a pool there? and toyon berries, dead ripe by now and
hanging by the fistful, put their redness in your riffles …?

Gerontic

Item in the paper:
'In people over sixty the
sweat glands have begun
to deteriorate.' It is
yet another touch
on the hair-trigger
of this horror at what
has been happening
to him.
          How quietly
the small disasters arrive
and form up in this
irreversible disaster
old age. Every change
now, is for the worse.
'There's no future in it,'
he jokes to a smooth-faced
young friend, knowing they belong
to different species now.

He'd been thinking
about the young waiter in
the Hemingway tale,
who declares, 'An old man
is a nasty thing.' The kid's
exasperated: it's closing
time, his girlfriend
is waiting for him. The old
man, the one remaining
patron, quite drunk, has,

with his dignity
intact, just ordered
another brandy. The older
of the two waiters defends
the old man, quietly
and well. The other, not
disputing him, serving
the old man his one more
brandy, sticks to
his own opinion.

He folds up the newspaper.
Nothing to be done
but make 'Spinoza's
laconic agreement to
conspire with necessity,'
phrasing he had copied
(from whom? he's forgotten)
years ago into a notebook.
As for the knowledge and
wisdom of old age, such as
they may be, their basis
and most of their substance
he had built up, well
before he was old, back
when thoughts and perceptions
came at propitious times
unsought-for, quick and clear....

Mid-July, down the back-country
streamside trail
he loved most, the stream
slow and low, mid-day
air quivering
above the scrub, how
he'd pour sweat, soak
his heavy belt clear through.

July 21, 1994

Back in 1946–47

We'd turn first to those poems by him,
when the new issue came out, though knowing
they would just be studies of flowers—
brief, accurate, vivid—different
individual flowers, their shapes, their
positions and balancings on their stems,
small movements special to them, the varying
gradations of light and shadow
to be watched for in their interiors—
quick-moving, elegant poems, though.

He was one of the crowd of us vets
on campuses right after the war.
He kept to the edges, was of us
but not among us. His laconic
observations—offered quietly with
his hands in his pockets as always
(we never saw him with a book)—were admired,
not least for their genial and ever-
inventive use of the meager stock
of the stale obscenities in soldier talk.

None of us could say just when
he left that campus, on its hill
above the then pleasant city,
across which we could see, through
the then clear air, the blue Rockies
looking near. You could find his poems
back there, in the library basement files—
that is, if the files still exist.

May, 1994

Two Pieces out of a Winter Morning

I. UP CLOSE

On the far side of the crossing
Where the stream swung under a cliff
There was a big boulder, roughly the shape
Of a bull bison lying down.

A low-leaning oak shades it in the heat
Of summers up there. Winter sunlight (often subtle,
As there, in its treatment of what it crosses)
Reached in and warmed it a bit on the south end.

It was a stopping-place. That day he only paused
And keeping his pack on leaned with a bare hand
On the shoulder of stone at the north end. The cold
Stored inside it from last night went into his palm.

He saw for the first time that the stone
With its dark iron tones, deep in chill shadow,
Bore a crop of lichens, round patches, with edgings,
Flower-like in many shades of subdued

Yet luminous grays. Among them grew irregular plots
Of moss, some olive-green and very bright, even
In that shade, some a fresh brownish green, in velvety
Low mounds: a sort of park for the eye to wander in

For a moment or so. He let be, those days, the enigma
He'd studied for years—the attraction that all
The boulders up here have exerted on him, in all
Their shapes and sizes: say, showing their backs

In the rapids and slow runs of the streams,
Or flood-crammed onto canyon floors, or poised,
Huge and single on the slopes (one over a pool
He used to fish), or choking the side-gulches,
Or standing here and there in the open grassy places,
Or paired and flanking the trail at one bend he knew.

2. OVER THE FENCE

You went in between big orange groves
On the way up there. The trees,
Standing in long straight rows
Each row and each tree in it
Spaced the same, were once
Skillfully tended. Neglected later,
Yellowing, some of them
Already dead, they were some more
Speculative real estate, though that morning
As he drove through they were still
Sending equidistant shadows
Aslant over the black-top, between which
The low-going sun had laid flush a row
Of wide palings, pure light: they hurt his eyes,
One after another flashing an instant
Before vanishing smoothly under the tires.

Mid-December, 1993

High Summer

She moved so fast
sometimes—in the house
and out and back in
in one rush—but unruffled—
just from her usual
abounding energy
that one time
the dog sat up
and began barking
from sheer excitement.

Under Cricket Music

A fragment

1

Crickets from where the hill is steep
And dark under the oaks across the street
Keep up a clear and brilliant *threep — threep — threep,*
    A little harsh, with a quick beat,
Filtering through trees the jounce of harness bells,
These late fall nights, somehow, from some place else —

2

Some time else. I remember, though,
Mainly the sound, with much else fallen away,
Leaving nostalgia with no place to go.
    A team heading home, end of the day.
Would the small bright bells chink from tugs, or hames,
    Or bridles — I don't know.
I cannot even recall the horses' names....

3

At a small hour I again awake;
In the live silence one cricket's creaking on
Slowly, now, muted, but without a break.
    He's quiet when I wake at dawn:
Trim bit of reality for in between
    Dreams, and oblivion,
That take their turns all night on the inner scene.

4

Oblivion that slides in, recedes,
Slides in, all the while floating all that is,
Is best of all — 'Come, sleep,' come dark that feeds
        Into the veins cool nothingness —
The old poets, broken, wrote their loveliest
        That the god might dip misdeeds,
Fears, all, in the deep sleep of the old psychopannychist —

5

And yet just yesterday I fought
Afternoon drowsiness off to watch how each
        Curt stroke of Nicholas of Cusa's thought
        Bore him on, into a bright reach
Where Infinite and Finite co-inhered
        And the mere world on a taut
And shining gossamer of wisdom reappeared....

6

A rocks-crawling-with-rattlers dream,
Dream where each act, as Clausewitz said of war,
Is simple, and very difficult; trout stream
        I know I've visited before
(But where?) flowing opaque with sewage; gray
        Steep vacant street, dark store
And office in a strange, vast city where I stray

7

Dread-filled, and what am I doing there —
And my son is a puny baby, putting by
His pitiful few possessions with great care
    Next to him, on the rug. As I
Laugh hard, he crawls off, thin-limbed, spirited,
    On his own, to disappear
Through a dark opening, sloping below his bed —

[left unfinished]

ca. 1979; August 23, 1996

Homage to Gensei

Last night I lay awake
From some sound in the night
And pictured I could take
(Knowing that I could not)
The firm and quiet way
Of the gentle monk Gensei,
Who watched from his Grass Hill
(Three hundred years away)
Beneath a favorite tree,
Or from his leaky hut,
Travels of crow, cloud, sail;
With some food and wine
Welcomed the always rare
Visit from old friends; wrote
His poems, though unwell
Much of the time; read; gave
Lessons, again while sick,
Kept clear of pedantry
(And all he wrote of it
Rings true of it today),
With his goose-foot walking stick
To keep him company
Took walks, kept his mind free
And agile as the air,
Transcending tragedy,
Under his bent old pine
With writing brush in hand
Quiet at close of day
Saw out the evening sun
Across the shadowy land.

~

Slight rustlings in a tree
And a slow car going by
Returned me to what's mine,
What it had all come to,
What I still had to do
With my own dwindling days.

Herders Moving a Flock Down Highway 395

A thousand sheep crowding the mountain road
Make it look like a dirty-foam-capped river
In this dim light. They've blocked the truck ahead.
His double chrome exhaust pipes snort and quiver.

He needs to be getting on, and so do I,
And all those headlights behind us, stopped at dawn.
The road is narrow, the mountain stops the eye
Rightward, thin air on the left goes on and on.

Sleepy, hatless, uncombed, after a night on the ground
In the clothes they're wearing, two herders amble
Behind the flock, and the three dogs in sight
Keep the flanks neat—make a rare laggard scramble.

What leads the flock is a burro, while a third
Man wades along in their midst—now and then waves
A bough torn from a bay tree over the herd.
Dew soaks their wool and the dark, fresh bay leaves.

Across the blat and clatter, through the daze
Of recent sleep he sees us apparitions
With a wide, flashing, and incurious gaze
Now that we creep past in our own conditions.

Now that we creep past in our own conditions
And catch in the dawn, along with the ancient moral
Of simple sheep, and shepherds, and our ambitions,
Reek of damp wool, pungency of torn laurel.

Early summer, 1982; August, 1996

A Memorial in the Neighborhood

It is a young oak tree and a stone
with a bronze plaque in it, for
a boy who lived all his life
in a house up the street from ours,
near the park entrance-road. He died in
his room over the garage, a suicide.

His mother had her memorial for him
placed on a piece of ground scraped bare
and packed hard, in the weedy area
at the upper end of the park,
between the creek and a trailhead
where you start out for the back-country.

We never knew, but knew of
the family. I glimpsed the father once—
handsome, dark-haired. Took off when the boy
was small, and the brothers grown
and gone; among the cousins and uncles
were artists and actors; some widely known.

The boy himself was a painter,
quiet and shyly friendly
the one time when I met him. After
his death we would see his mother
now and then, for a year or so,
then she sold the house and left.

In her grief (I'm supposing) she left the choice
of a stone and the placement of the plaque
to the stonemason. It's a puzzle
that the man should botch that simple job: why choose
an unshapely, lopsided stone? and then set
the plaque in violently askew?

Later, somebody in the mix
of the people using a public park—some one
of those whose furtive doings make for
that slight, pervading taint of evil
in the air of a park: as here, over the boulders, the creek,
and trees and grassy open places—someone

took the trouble to batter a big chunk
off that poor specimen of a stone.
So it stands there now, in a place where boulders
of all sizes abound in a variety of fine
rounded shapes, tablet shapes, shapes of mountains
in miniature with ledges, hollows, cliffs; and then,

a back-country peak stands over us all
down here, in our houses deep in trees, and for
situation, and shape, this peak is a match
for Fuji, I swear; and mornings, ocean air,
evenings, canyon air, moves in the trees here, it's all
a garden here, violated variously, but a garden.

~

The words the mother chose for
the plaque could not be more plain.

This tree was planted
in memory of

then the name and the two dates—one morning
I stood there and did the subtraction
in my head, getting the number of years,
months, and days that the boy lived.

The young oak has grown tall now, straight-stemmed,
well above the thick stakes it is held between,
its crown shapely, its leaves rich dark green
with the special shine all living things have in
their youth. Around it its elders lean, in their contortions
from crowding, as is their nature; fallen limbs under them.

~

This Christmas, as on every Christmas,
now, for fourteen years, decorations have appeared
on the tree. I went up there early
one weekday morning, when nobody
would be around. I wanted the time
to study them and not get stared at.

A huge bow of shiny red plastic is tied
on the trunk this time. Globes covered with some
shiny synthetic fiber hang from the branches:

twenty-three red ones, two blue, and in no
discernible arrangement, have hung there weeks, now,
past the holiday season, fraying and fading, in

this winter's rainstorms. They'll be taken down,
always have been. They don't get forgotten about:
the choice, arrangement, and handling of them do not
matter, Taste doesn't matter, behind them being
the grief that stays on, alive, under whatever
the rest may be by which living gets done.
There to be visited, on its occasions.

December 18, 1994

Three Studies from Two Days

The Upper North Fork, Matilija, 1986

1. LATE IN THE DAY

Part of the thin shadow
   of a weed stem
Cutting the trail solidified
   into a lizard
And ran away, still
   shadow-colored.

2. PHOTOGRAPHING AN UNCOMMON WILDFLOWER

Now it's been found.
Shapely and fresh dark blue,
   Fine-stemmed, neat-leaved,
   On the baked-white ground—
A subject, magnified, swaying there
   In its prime,
   A foot away,
   Difficult still
To catch, on this dry, stony, steep hill
   (That would kill
   Its garden cousins in no time).

You lean, shaken with late-in-the-day
   Fatigue, and with one knee
   Wedged between rocks, one eye
   At the eye-piece, water-blurred
   By the hot breeze,
   The other shut tight, by
   Sweat and two crawling flies
   Whose cohorts whirl above—
   You'll wait till it holds still …

Unlikely place for both flower and you
To choose (all but absurd
For you to love).
Still, there you both are, each in your way
(By reflex) hopeful, too.
The least breeze shakes your prize,
In its brief stay,
As naturally
As fatigue and more shake you
At sixty-two....

3. THE LIZARDS OF LIZARD FLAT

Just ahead of us they run, stop, run, stop, their transit
Building a structure light and elegant,
Jointed with pauses,

Extending itself in segments (with time out
For slewing sidewise to look back at the humans)
Like shooting bamboo.

A Pull-out by the Sespe

For years this stream ran clear.
I'd fish it alone, all day.
Then came the long drought. Now
we stand in the familiar
dirt pull-out, drinking coffee.
When the off-and-on breeze hits,
two young cottonwoods begin stirring
on the near bank, half their branches
still green, the others yellow.
We watch their all-over shivery
hard twinkling leaves
throwing off flakes and
sharp flicks of light, at all
angles, continuously: all the while
the leaves send out their sounds
of running water, as if in recollection
of the stream they grew up by; which is
now silent—dusty stones, weeds. Someone
has hung a jumbo empty
Frito bag carefully
on a bush on the far bank.

Away from the Road

I

FOR A GREAT BASIN BRISTLECONE PINE

For picking a high place,
unsheltered; using shattered rock
to thread roots through to the poor and
shallow soil; strong at extremes: in
relentless winds, only a few
cushion-plants for company
on the last ridge twisting up, up
aslant in thin bright-blue air,
slow swerves in its multiple
twistings, in its grain its warm
colors staying fresh in this dry cold
through the centuries—tree that is one wild contortion
from its sprawled-out clenched-down root system
half-bared by erosion, to the snag
of its tip, single existence in
among existences which sustain
and assail it at the same time: what else
is there to be found—you cannot
imagine the nothingness of the before
and after—you get no further than
the silence of stone, of a standing bristlecone
in the terrific fixity of its achieved exertions.
Still there is a certain casualness in
its leaning into open space, and
in its reach for air and light up here
there's eagerness not anguish. You see it
in the jaunty half-twirl of
the barkless twig at the top.

2

FOR THE ASPENS AND COTTONWOODS
UP ON BIG PINE CREEK

Just the one branch lifts,
hesitates, and subsides
in small splashings of light.

~

Half-waking in hemlock shade
he lies listening, eyes still shut:
is it the voice of a young woman
that he hears upstream? But it goes on
earnestly, eagerly, the tones
explanatory, never pausing
for a breath, never varying
in volume: they are water-sounds.
He opens his eyes and sees
three aspens full of light,
one of them against the dark
of an old pine, all three quiet
at the moment. Onset of boredom
both with the sounds of the creek
upstream and the aspens alike
involuntarily declaring themselves.
A faint breeze that hasn't yet
reached him strikes the trees, making
a kind of silent clinking
with fine spikes of light from
the leaves in movement....
Fairly good logs can be made

from aspens for barns and sheds,
also a good quality pulp, though
as fenceposts they rot out fast.
What they are best for is
catching light in high air
and sending it uselessly out. When
he walks over to these three,
he leaves the daylight,
and stands inside aspen light.

3

FOR THE UTAH JUNIPER

They find in ruins of the Anasazi
(the name in Navajo: the Vanished
Ones, Old Ones, Old Enemies)
juniper roof-beams, still sound,
juniper-bark torches. Slow growers,
roots fed into sandstone, the junipers
dot the scene to the horizon, holding their dark
over the pale rock; in summer light
lightless; grave green the year round,
stolid; tragic trees, for the long haul,
their coarse black blunt flame-shapes
leaving the sandy canyon bottoms
to the cottonwoods, those gleamers
and glisteners of brief summer,
quickly undone, stripped and stilled—
non-participants in the bitter winters.

The Fox

In the year 1954 of a bygone era

Fall came and he took a leave
(certain he could not sit through
another graduate class—not
yet), wrote a bit, taught one class—
he liked to teach, they needed
the money he put with what
she earned at her office job.

He'd fish the small stream that ran
below the cliffs at the edge
of town. They ate what he caught;
ate the blackberries, soft-ripe
large ones, that grew at streamside.
They made some blackberry wine,
once, from a small bucketful.

And sometimes he went hunting.
He found a good single-shot
.22 in a cluttered
second-hand store outside town.
It was old but well cared-for—
smelt of gun-oil, and the bore
was bright, clear of corrosion.

Through friends who rented one floor
of a farmhouse out from town
a mile or so, he'd obtained
permission from the owner
to hunt on his land—squirrels,
the man said, had been raiding
the cornfield he'd not yet picked.

He parked in the yard at dawn
on the first day he hunted
and walked up a wagon road
that wound through leafless gray woods.
The trees were unfamiliar.
Once he had edged in among them—
he'd heard a squirrel chatter.

The trunks stood close together.
How the land lay further in,
he could neither see nor guess.
Another squirrel chattered
further in. He retreated
to the road, and felt relieved.
As he went on, the woods thinned.

In a clearing by the road
stood a small persimmon tree,
leafless in the reddish light,
the first one he'd ever seen.
He walked up the grassy slope
for a closer look. In the quiet
the bright fruit hung motionless.

He never saw another person,
nor a sign of one, back here,
nor even any livestock.
He had come out here in part,
he now knew, for the stillness.
There were no noises here—
only sounds, to be listened for.

~

Once his wife had come along
with him and a friend, hunting
at dusk, just outside the town.
The friend brought down a squirrel,
it ran off, he and the friend
lunged after it, stumbling, on
rocks and downed wood in deep leaves.

He recalled her clear laughter—
clear of derision: to her
the chase was pure comedy....
That night they ate squirrel he
had shot. Like chicken, they said.
But no—an alien tang
which cooking, and seasoning,

could never quite rid it of
caused them an uneasiness
that, though slight, had persisted
like the strong scent of the fresh
pelt still in the kitchen. And
bits of the underfur, pale,
hard to see, stuck to the meat....

On one late November day
he came up the wagon-track
through the stands of long-bare trees,
mild sunlight came slanting in,
the different trunk-shadows
ahead of him were soft gray.
He stepped through shafts of the light.

He heard the far, crashing sounds
of squirrels making long leaps
through the leaves from trunk to trunk.
The persimmon tree stood now
stripped of fruit—the strong, thin twigs
stayed bent. The road left the woods
and turned, to follow the edge

of a bluff that overlooked
the farmer's bottom-land field—
light streaming through the ripe crop
made it buckskin-colored now.
A creek ran past the far edge
of the field, big sycamores
on the near bank caught the light.

The far bank, though, steep and dark,
dense with trees and undergrowth,
looked cold, dank, in its deep shade.
A breeze came up as he watched.
He heard the rattle and rasp
of the dry, sharp-edged, stiff leaves
of the corn. He walked on down

watching for any movement
that was not caused by the breeze,
went past the head of the field
to the creek. The breeze died down.
He'd seen crows, but no squirrels
except one pair that vanished,
high in an old sycamore.

~

He sat under that same tree,
on the stream-bank, his feet
dangling. He could hear water
going past slowly, hidden
under leaves, among the stones.
A clear, crescent-shaped pool lay
along the bank, just upstream.

The bank there was undercut.
The massive trunk of the tree
let down a tangle of roots
over the pool. The water,
motionless, mirrored the roots.
Leaves on the pale bottom-stones
lay draped, their colors still fresh.

For those few moments the place
had magical properties.
This stayed clear and fresh, for him,
from then on—the time of day,
and the season, did their part
no doubt, and that cold, dank slope,
and the bright field at his back.

The air stayed quiet. The day
would soon be cooling, a slow
flow of air would wind downstream,
its chill seep into the folds
of his clothes; but this air still
was mild. As he watched, the light
weakened on the chalky-white

undersides of two big limbs
the tree had sent out, level
and winding, over the creek.
The limbs remained motionless.
He listened to a trickle
of water dripping over
a rock ledge, somewhere below.

He heard a dry, light rustling
far up past the bend upstream.
For all its slightness, the sound
came to him clearly, the air
having been still for so long.
He looked upstream and waited.
What appeared around the bend

was a gray fox. It was tired,
and came on, down the center
of the streambed, at a slow
steady trot with its head low,
its tail level with its back.
It held its eyes straight ahead
as it drew near where he sat.

They were eyes dulled by fatigue.
Mud had soaked its legs, belly,
and flanks, and matted the long,
fine fur of the underside
of its plume. The fox went by
sparing itself the effort
of a glance aside at him,

and rounded the bend downstream.
He listened till the dwindling
rustle of leaves had died out,
and then he kept on listening
in the new stillness around
for some minutes. Well, he thought,
he has built up a good lead.

He pictured the fox moving
through the coming dusk and dark
downstream toward settled country.
He could not convincingly
see where the fox then might go.
He was getting up to leave
when he first heard the foxhounds.

The far-off, varied baying,
oddly melodious, came
drifting in through the stillness.
—Yes, they're a long way upstream.
And this creekbed that the fox
chose for its course, is a choice
course for a pack of foxhounds.

He did not stay on to watch
the pack go by. He gathered
his gun and rucksack and left,
glad he had brought a flashlight.
He knew this breed was tireless.
They'd stream past, wild-eyed, long ears
flapping, tails up and waving….

~

One mild spring evening two years
later, as the dusk thickened
toward darkness in the soft air,
he came back down to his car
as he'd done five or six times
since the day he saw the fox;
but this was for the last time.

He still carried the rifle,
from habit, and his liking
for it. But lately he'd come
just to take the track up there
between the trees, to the bluff,
then down to the creek, to see
how things were out there that day.

He had done all you did for
the degree. They were leaving
that place, for one with no woods
but plenty of cactus; then
on to a place with ocean,
and mountains. They settled there,
knew the mountain trails, the streams,

knew shores after winter storms
left them stony, driftwood-strewn;
knew the salt-marshes, russet
in winter, where shore-birds came
from the far north. Certain days
they've had there stay in his mind,
none more detailed, none clearer,

than the day he saw the fox.

August 11, 1996

Note: The ancient Greeks saw that such places were sacred and had a goddess. You disregarded her at your peril. She was Artemis, and as my *Oxford Classical Dictionary* words it, 'her proper sphere is the earth, and specifically the uncultivated parts, forests, and hills, where wild beasts are plentiful.' Not to have been able to spend sufficient time appropriately in such places would have made me waste away in the other phases of my life.

Reflecting Pool

Time: the middle hours of a day in late December

*I, who love walking, and who always hated riding, who am fond of
some society, but never had spirits that would endure a great deal, could
not, as you perceive, be better situated.*

— WILLIAM COWPER, THE LETTERS…,
(EVERYMAN LIBRARY NO. 774, p. 201)

The sound of a waterfall down below
had made him turn off the trail; now
he was working his way down,
crouching to get under low
branches, shoving aside or
snapping off the smaller stuff,
his boots skidding, his cap
snatched off once, his pack
twice lodging against a limb,
stopping him dead with a jolt,
making him bend even lower
to go on. He was sliding sidewise
when the falls and its big pool
came into sight. He was here
for the first time.
                  Just below him,
a boulder sunk into the slope would do
for a seat with the vantage-point
he wanted, once he'd found stones
to fill a wide cleft in it
and cleared away some intruding
thin branches and twigs.

~

He eased off his pack and sat, still
catching his breath. He'd come out
near the foot of the pool, where the ripples
were pushing upstream in shallow arcs
evenly spaced. The waterfall was bright white,
small and steady. It dropped from the V
formed by a pair of big, clean boulders
up above. *And it can't be improved upon,*
he thought.
    He was out of sight
from the trail above, and from the far bank
where the slope was steep and the trees
and the undergrowth too dense for a hiker
to force. He was alone with the place.

He worked out of his pack the box
he'd squeezed a big sandwich into.
He positioned three river-stones on
the slope, to set the box upon. It was almost
level. He drew out his thermos, steadied it
between his boots, and with the edge
of a piece of flat, thin sandstone
that had broken cleanly, loosened
and levelled the soil between two rocks,
unscrewed the thermos cup, and pressed
the rounded bottom into the ground,
rotating it back and forth, to make a socket
for the cup to stand in; and then slowly
filled the cup with coffee. He replaced
the stopper and laid the thermos on the slope,

its base against a boulder. There was no spot
to stand it on. Then he ate, and watched
the yellow leaves revolving at the lower end
of the pool. They went counterclockwise. Those
in front of him travelled upstream, then swerved
back across the water, rejoining the main current
where it drove against, then along, the far bank. Then,
slowing and swinging on back around, the leaves
came toward him on the quiet water. Alder leaves,
brilliant where sunlit, bright in the shadows.

The whole place lay held in the water-fall noise.

~

He would come up alone to see
what the day here would be like
this time, on this or the other
branch of the little river.
He had been doing so since the days
when few people came up here. He still
liked the hidden edge of danger
here, and the change from the useful
and not so useful routines
at home. As he walked along
taking in things around, his mind
might, on its own, work at some
persisting difficulty in some of
his reading, or in some writing,
and the lacking thing arrive by itself,

he getting it down without delay,
having learned that his memory could
not be trusted with it. The other day
he had read in Aubrey that Hobbes
when at work on *Leviathan*
often took walks and kept a pen
and inkhorn in the head of
his walking-staff, so that when 'a
notion darted,' he could write it
down, on the spot.

       — Coming up here
was no escape from any
bad time he was having. He'd learned
that the bad time tagged along.

He liked walking up here
with his wife, with his sons,
with a friend or friends.
When you are here with others,
the place is the occasion and
being with others is the event.
Those were good times.
Memories of them stayed
lively. Always his need
to go up here alone was
for the place itself. In time
it became a physical need.

～

Within the water-noise he was hearing the *buzz-buzz*
of some small bird. He couldn't identify it. Now, still
buzzing, the bird approached in stages, keeping hidden,
causing no movements of the leaves that might
give away its position, but keeping on the move and
both scolding him and sending out the news
of his presence here.
                              No voices, no other
sounds from above of people going by
up on the trail. The U.S. Forest Service built
the trail, he reminded himself. Trail that leads on
into these mountains — and then on back
down to the narrow dirt road, that takes
you down to the locked gate, where the blacktop
begins, that takes you winding back
down toward.... His sense of things here today
was temporary. Well, so was any sense of things.
He thought of the phrase 'the lightning flash
of reality' in a van Gogh letter.

                              ~

                              One soft
      spring day many years back, he was on
      the trail along the main fork, nearing
      a stretch of the stream he considered his.
      You reached it by a hard-to-make-out
      way through the scrub. He told no one
      about it, he'd never seen anyone else

on it. The stream was beautiful, and it had
many trout in it.
        Out of view in his pack
was his new pack-rod, and his other tackle,
all of it first rate. It had taken him years
to get it all together, one item
at a time, mostly. The day before,
a dozen trout-flies had been delivered
Air Mail, Special Delivery, just
in time. They rested now in the clear box
they came in, next to his reel, in the pack
(he kept all his tackle out of sight
until he got down to the stream)
and his mind was on them. They had come
from Livingston, Montana. They were tied
by local women, mostly middle-aged,
sitting at long benches. One year
there had been a photograph of them
in the catalog. The flies were packed
and shipped (by another such woman,
maybe) upon the arrival of his order,
check enclosed. The money it was
that brought them. His dozen
Royal Wulffs had come bobbing down
from Dan Bailey's on a rivulet
of money — liquidity, that was
the lingo; cash flow, that his job had
turned into; job he was, well, spending
his life in. He saw the whole
country afloat on money. All things were

soaked in it (including money
itself) so that from them money
could be squeezed. A great convenience,
no doubt. Too bad about its power
to pervert.... *On such a day
as this, in such a place — what a topic,*
he'd thought, his eye alert once again
to any slight change portending
danger to the place: this narrow
road, grassy and weedy down
the middle, dwindling vaguely into
the trail up ahead, was a great threat....

He had turned off and made his way
down toward the stream, easing through
the stiff, abrasive chaparral, clambering
over boulders, crossing several gullies.
He was fifty miles from home. Inventing
the wheel, Ford Madox Ford had written,
was where we had gone wrong. He'd laughed
when he read that. It had come to seem,
some forty years later, his consideration
of it fitfully persisting, plausible.
He tried to recall the title of that book.

~

He was midway through lunch when he saw
the quick indistinct movement, deep in the pool.
Getting out his binoculars he soon found

the two trout: six-inchers, like twins.
The floating leaves made excellent cover for
the pair moving slowly below them. Their bodies,
being the green of the clear green sunny water,
looked translucent, their shadows were inconspicuous
among the shadows of the leaves and of the flat
stones on the sandy bottom. He watched the pair
hover, and then cruise, with an easy flick
of fin shifting direction, assured and
unhurried among the shifting pillars of
the shadows of floating alder leaves.

He no longer fished. His tackle stayed in its cabinet.
One day soon he'd divide it among his sons.
They could cut cards to settle any disputes. Now
he was content with just coming up here.

It was one of those places that has
a radiance of its own. You could see it
when your state of attention was right.

~

The whole pool was lying in one cold shadow.
He replaced the empty thermos and box
in the pack, worked the binoculars back
into their case, and passing the strap over
his head, hung it over his right shoulder so that
the binoculars rested on his left hip. He hoisted
the pack and shrugged into it, buckling

the waist-belt, tightening the shoulder-straps.
The pack had some weight to it. He always carried
what he would need if for any reason
he should have to spend the night up here.
He secured the binoculars to the waist-belt
with a thong, buckled the chest-strap, turned
away from the pool and its waterfall, fought
his way back up to the trail, and once again
headed back down into what lay outspread below.

December 19, 1994

Note: The title of Ford's book is *Great Trade Route*.

A Sip of the Manzana

A long time since he'd been here,
and now, it was against
doctor's orders ('… and stay out
of the heat …'). He had come up
through the deep sand of the trail,
at mid-day, through the dry
fiery air summers bring
up here. Back of him lay
the campground, where he'd parked,
two horse-trailers nearby,
and a single, sagging, small tent.

Now he slogged along, through
sand (loosened by hooves)
hot and white in the white
blaze of over-head sun,
and no movement of air,
his face heating up,
his skin staying dry—
only ten minutes
to the grove of big oak,
digger pine, cottonwood,
and the slow-shifting, black-
shadow shelter they gave.

Near a scatter of boulders
with air tremors above them,
in the dead grasses and weeds
and low, twisting shrubs
drought-stricken and prickly

on the rise he chose,
he sat eating his lunch,
taking drinks of ice-water
from a small thermos.
The plan: he would use
ten minutes to get here,
say twenty to eat
and take in what was here,
then ten more to return,
then drive back to the cool
blue of the coast. He stuck
with the plan.

       From his spot
on the rise, he looked at—no,
watched, a young digger pine,
slender, airy; sunlight slid
up and down its needles
whenever they moved. Nearby
stood its tall forebear, hung
with old, long-opened cones
in heavy, dark clumps,
their scales tipped with claws.
Beside it three sycamores
towered, limbs sprawling out
in the air, and a cottonwood
flickered—its glossy leaves
swivelling on those thin, flat
stems set at right angles
to the leaf surfaces—

they made a light clatter
as a lazy air movement
eased its way through the boughs,
and the digger pines hissed
and the sounds of the river
out of sight from this rise
came in more distinctly.
Now and then a bird crossed
from one tree to another
while keeping the silence
birds observe at mid-day
in the midsummer up here.

At his feet, under grass-stems
low-leaning, or snapped off
cleanly at the base, lying
full length in the dirt,
still sleek and bright-pale
in this shade, lay last year's
weather-discolored
cottonwood leaves, their
high polish ruined, though
some still showed as luminous
where brushed now by light
sifting down through the boughs
of the oak just above him.
The few oak leaves among them
had kept their dull brown—
weather-proof, tough—their
hard, convex surfaces

with clean, scalloped edges
gripping the ground
with the just-visible
sharp hooks at their tips.

Once a doctor, treating
some other affliction, had told him
'No alcohol' and thereupon
at the end of the day,
he would take one swallow
of no substitute, but
absolutely the real thing,
straight from the bottle,
in its full—if transient—
restorative powers
(then he let the ritual
lapse).—What had Saint Ben
said, in his shining iambics,
but the whole truth?—'In small
proportions we just
beauties see: and in
short measures, life
may perfect be....'

On that rise, with the great trees
around and above him
with their sounds and movements
and with them the distant,
fitful sound of the river,
he had entered a state

*he'd not gone there to be in
(if he had, he would never
have entered it), and of which
he was not aware—was not able
to be—while in it. It was
something he'd know of,
and be able to visit,
        only afterward.*

Names of Trout Flies

Out of his mail, which was heavy
with catalogs, he pulled the early
spring numbers of the catalogs
of Orvis and Dan Bailey,
and on this gray day of this
bleak February turned to the pages
of splendid photographs in color
of the trout flies. Dan Bailey's
number lined them up in rows
of six, stacked seven high. Inset
on one page was a photograph
of a vast brown meadow backed by
mountains, light blue and with many peaks
tipped and streaked with snow. Barely
showing at the far edge of the meadow
was a thread-thin scratch of light:
the river over there.
                The front half
of a heavy trout in close-up, speckled
jet-black on light green, loomed
in an inset on one Orvis page of nymphs.
A hand suspended the trout just above
a blur of rapid water. One clear drop
of that water was hanging midway
along the jutting jaw of the trout,
another from one knuckle of the hand.
The fly that the big trout had taken
had been removed. The hand was about
to release the trout.

~

Glanced at,
they formed a fine, small spectacle,
the rows of trout flies. On impulse
he made a rough count: three hundred
or so flies across eight pages
in the Orvis. Dan Bailey showed,
across thirteen pages, around four
hundred fifty. The little order form
in the corner of one page was for a book
of patterns and materials for more
than a thousand classic and contemporary
flies.
        Without their names, the trout flies
would just be their exotic materials
tied together and trimmed — feathers
 (Guinea, Peacock, Silver Pheasant, Jungle
Cock, etc.), hair (Northern Whitetail,
Coastal Deer, Yearling Elk, Antelope,
Moose Mane, etc.), specimens of fur,
of silk floss, of chenille (Regular,
Tinsel, Short Flash, Long Flash, Ultra),
French Wire (gold, silver, copper, in
Small, Medium, and Large), and so on.
The trout flies have their names, though.
Hard to match them for liveliness and
unexpectedness in certain sequences
or pairings the names come in: bright
miniature assemblages of the language
into not-quite-compositions, with
their fleeting intimations, so that

each fly has its aureole, hovering
just out of reach with just sufficient
resistance to a filled-out meaning
you could take hold of.
                    The names
entranced him when he was a boy,
he remembered. He was pausing here and there
at the name beneath the photograph
of a trout fly in its row. Some names
had their accidental beauty, some
an unaccountable oddity (e.g.
Bead Head Blood Mohair); some
a satisfying plainness (Joe's Hopper,
this with the most recessive of
aureoles). He turned to the first section
of Orvis flies and began sampling.
Pale Evening Dun (his favorite, in
the beauty category), Halfback
Nymph (a combination that can't
be imagined), Rat Face McDougal, Green
Drake, Light Cahill, Hare's Ear, Blue Dun,
Dark Spruce, Royal Wulff, Grizzly
Wulff, Quill Gordon (one of the oldest
of patterns), Yellow Stimulator,
Marabou Muddler, Royal Trude, Elk
Hair Humpy, Blonde Wulff (the family
of Wulffs is large), The Professor,
Green Double Humpy, Renegade,
Female Adams, Adams Dry, Hairwing
Bluewing Olive, Silver Doctor (another

old one), Golden Fluttering Stone,
Cow Dung (he could never reconstruct
pathways by which the mind in search
of a name for a new trout fly might
arrive at Cow Dung; however, Cow Dung
it was, for what is a still serviceable
old trout fly), Blue Quill, Bitch Creek,
Cream Crane Fly, Olive Peeking Nymph
(vivid little almost-picture). He looks up
again, thinking of the light skittering
across fast water, the calm shine
of water full of leaf reflections
at a bend; the sudden cold clamped
into his legs through his waders, the almost
alarming force of this particular current
as he entered some wide water moving
majestically in near-perfect silence
through one mountain meadow; pool
under a single leaning tree, white uproar
in the narrows, and he balancing there
on a boulder....
   Looking down again:
it was the Irresistible catching his eye,
then Zug Bug, and South Fork Sally,
and Gray Fox, Hare's Ear Flashback,
Parmachene Belle (another of the old
ones, still good), Madame X Rubberlegs,
Grizzly King, Heavy Bitch Creek, Brown
Matuka, Gray Ghost, Black Leech,
Adult Blue Damsel, Royal Stimulator,

Brassie, Spruce Fly, Babine Special,
Jack Scott, and the Royal Coachman
 (striking handiwork of the man of
that title who served Queen Victoria).

He got down a brittle, yellowing
1949 paperback and located the page
displaying "The Preferred Flies
in 1892." All but two were listed
in his new catalogs.
                    He himself
in the last eleven of some sixty
years of fishing, used just one fly,
in one size: the Royal Wulff
 (a variant, by the master
Lee Wulff, of the Royal Coachman)
barbless, size 14. The other flies
he had chosen over the years —
dry flies, wet flies, in many sizes,
streamers and nymphs and muddlers
and the big stoneflies — flies for various
times of day in every phase of
the trout season, lay shut tight,
each kind in its own compartment
in a clear box, the boxes stacked
in the dark of their cabinet.
Whether the trout took his Royal Wulff
or not, he had been satisfied.
He'd caught enough trout. If, now
and then, he took and let go another,

he admired as always the all-out
startled indignant struggle of a wild
trout, even a small one. (Planted trout—
pellet-fed, soft-bodied from a life of
finning in one place side by side in hatchery
ponds—he shunned.)
                              In the last two seasons
he had left his tackle at home,
content with walking along a stream
by himself, content with a leisurely
survey of things, with the occasional
prolonged observation of this
or that; with sitting still.
                              To do
otherwise now, to take up active
fishing, would be like taking up
years later one of those books
which, as he read it, became
the signal event of that time
in his life. And such a book, once read,
had then become (while his mind
went on to other books and other
concerns) an occupant, vivid and
quiet in him. If one day years later
he took down the book and read
into it a little way, he'd find it was
still alive there in him. There were only
a few such books. The physical
book, the one that got dusty,
he would dust, and put back on its shelf.

~

He became aware, belatedly, that
a long narrow elegant isosceles
triangle of blazing sunlight
had been lengthening across the carpet
from the lower pane in the door
behind him, and had just arrived
at the far edge. The room had filled
with an early dusk of its own. The afternoon
had gone by, and he eased himself
out of his chair, dropping the catalogs
onto the catalogs sprawling in their basket.

Late February, 1995

A Portrait

… she wakes, and with the same
quick start and buoyancy
heads without hesitation
along her usual ways—those
trim routines she fashions
through ordinary days—
yet in an instant, game
for the unscheduled jaunt,
spur-of-the-moment spree.

So far as I can see
she's lived her life out free,
somehow, of the bad passions
(but knows well—forgivingly,
I've learned—the ones in me);
free of the wants that claw
and gnaw at others so
for this and that; has no
taint of that vanity,
ambition for her sons.

She's no worrier. Is brave,
those close to her can attest,
as her youngest son knows best,
whose life she dived to save
in the Rogue—a fast river
well-named from those it drowned.

She's quick to understand
the good that comes to hand
in the course of things, for what
it's worth. Her gaiety
at any flash of wit
confirms its quality.

And I saw just last night
her yet again fresh delight
at seeing the moon rise …

August 22, 1996

Author's Notes

FROM THE NOTE TO

TREE MEDITATION AND OTHERS (1970)

The poems are descriptive meditations rather than meditative descriptions—I mean that they are first and last about subjects, not objects, despite what may be appearance to the contrary. They arose usually when I had some time to myself, which perhaps gives them their pre- or post-social character, and they are put as plainly as I could manage.

FROM THE NOTE TO *IN PLAIN AIR* (1982)

Years pass and there continues in me a preoccupation with what it is to be in the physical universe, with its always individual near-at-hand doings and beings, human and otherwise; the whole show shading off into immensity and vagueness, and (however splendid or frightful or dull or, ultimately, unimaginably strange) with its bare unrelenting factuality hurtling along impassively as it does, in a kind of final dignity. Some sense of this preceded by a long time the writing of the poems, I suppose, and has something to do with their unreconstructed realism and particularity.

Something else. Among the new poems are poems I wouldn't let out by themselves but that—like an "openwork" line in a stanza—make their contribution to the ensemble: what counts for me in any collection is less the individual poem than the individual life, finding its way somehow, anyhow, directly and otherwise, into the whole work....

About the Author

Alan Stephens was born December 19, 1925, in Greeley, Colorado. He grew up on the family farm there, and served in the U.S. Army Air Corps. Thanks to the G.I. Bill, he attended Colorado State Teacher's College (now the University of Northern Colorado), the University of Colorado at Boulder, the University of Denver, and the University of Missouri. He received bachelor's and master's degrees from DU, and a Ph.D. from Missouri.

Stephens taught English at Arizona State University from 1954 to 1960, with a year at Stanford on a fellowship (1956–1957). He joined the faculty at the University of California, Santa Barbara, in 1960 and remained there until his retirement in 1989, except for a year at DU (1967–1968). He was a founding faculty member of the College of Creative Studies at UCSB.

He was married for 60 years to Frances Stephens. They raised three sons. He died July 21, 2009, at home in Santa Barbara. He may be found in his verses.

Editor's Note

This selection is drawn from the *Collected Poems*, but also includes a few of the unpublished poems Stephens circulated privately over the years, and one that appeared only in a periodical. The arrangement is chronological, for the most part. The unpublished poems are grouped with their published contemporaries.

Different versions of certain poems appeared in various books and in a compilation Stephens made in the 1990's. The revisions were always slight, except for omissions from *The Heat Lightning* (1967), a very limited edition, when selections were republished in *Tree Meditation and Others* (1970). From all the variants, I have chosen what seemed to me the best versions, favoring the originals when in doubt. In some poems, I accepted certain revisions but not others.

I made some changes in punctuation, spelling, and italicization, but I have preserved Stephens's idiosyncratic use of single quotation marks. In a few poems I revised phrasing a little, or deleted a word or a short passage. These revisions were based on an early manuscript (the sonnets "The Other Runner" and "... continued"), on revisions Stephens penciled into his copy of *Goodbye Matilija* ("Dream Vision," "After-words"), or on my judgment of what he would have welcomed ("The Open World," "The Summer," "Elegy: The Old Man," "Tree Meditation," "Thinking of Roethke," "Third Deposition," "And the Fat One ...," "Lion Camp," "Study of Wild Oats #2," "After-words," "The White Boat," "Under Cricket Music," "A Portrait"). In making that difficult judgment, and in other respects, I was glad to have the counsel of John Wilson, John Ridland, Tim Stephens, Robyn Bell, Bob Blaisdell, and Jace Turner.

I thank Dan Stephens as well, for his brotherly support.

—A.A.S.